"You wouldn't mind people thinking that we're going out with each other?" He cleared his throat. *"Dating...?"*

"Don't get the wrong idea," Claire said hurriedly. "I don't *want* to date anybody. And if I did, it wouldn't be my new boss. But if it's the solution to your...um... personal issue that I accidentally managed to get involved in today, I'm quite happy to go along with people *thinking* that we might be dating."

Tom was staring at her. "It might work both ways," he said slowly.

"How?"

"A new, unattached and attractive woman in town is not going to go unnoticed in a small town like this. If it gets around that *we're* getting to know each other, nobody's going to hit on you."

A silence fell between them that stretched on.

And on.

Or maybe it was just Claire's attention had caught so completely on something Tom had said that she wasn't hearing anything else.

He thought she was *attractive*?

Dear Reader,

One of the things I love the most about writing is being able to set a story in a place that is special to me.

Kaikoura is a small seaside town on the east coast of New Zealand's South Island—just a couple of hours from where I live.

It's famous for dramatic scenery, renowned gardens, baby seals and being the best place in New Zealand to see whales.

I've squeezed all these features into this book with my lovely characters Tom and Claire, who absolutely deserve the perfect ending to their story.

Happy reading!

Alison xxx

THEIR FAKE DATE RESCUE

ALISON ROBERTS

MEDICAL ROMANCE

If you purchased this book without a cover you should be aware that this book is stolen property. It was reported as "unsold and destroyed" to the publisher, and neither the author nor the publisher has received any payment for this "stripped book."

Harlequin® MEDICAL ROMANCE

ISBN-13: 978-1-335-99319-9

Their Fake Date Rescue

Copyright © 2025 by Alison Roberts

All rights reserved. No part of this book may be used or reproduced in any manner whatsoever without written permission.

Without limiting the author's and publisher's exclusive rights, any unauthorized use of this publication to train generative artificial intelligence (AI) technologies is expressly prohibited.

This is a work of fiction. Names, characters, places and incidents are either the product of the author's imagination or are used fictitiously. Any resemblance to actual persons, living or dead, businesses, companies, events or locales is entirely coincidental.

For questions and comments about the quality of this book, please contact us at CustomerService@Harlequin.com.

TM and ® are trademarks of Harlequin Enterprises ULC.

Harlequin Enterprises ULC
22 Adelaide St. West, 41st Floor
Toronto, Ontario M5H 4E3, Canada
www.Harlequin.com

Printed in U.S.A.

Alison Roberts has been lucky enough to live in the South of France for several years recently but is now back in her home country of New Zealand. She is also lucky enough to write for the Harlequin Medical Romance line. A primary school teacher in a former life, she later became a qualified paramedic. She loves to travel and dance, drink champagne, and spend time with her daughter and her friends. Alison Roberts is the author of over one hundred books!

Books by Alison Roberts

Harlequin Medical Romance

A Tale of Two Midwives

Falling for Her Forbidden Flatmate
Miracle Twins to Heal Them

Daredevil Doctors

Forbidden Nights with the Paramedic
Rebel Doctor's Baby Surprise

Morgan Family Medics

Secret Son to Change His Life
How to Rescue the Heart Doctor

Paramedics and Pups

The Italian, His Pup and Me

Therapy Pup to Heal the Surgeon
City Vet, Country Temptation
Paramedic's Reunion in Paradise
Midwife's Three-Date Rule

Visit the Author Profile page
at Harlequin.com for more titles.

**Praise for
Alison Roberts**

"The love story is built up slowly but surely with just the right amount of passion and tenderness.
This novel will tug at your heartstrings and give you hope in miracles. All romance readers need to grab a copy of this terrific tale ASAP."

—*Harlequin Junkie* on
A Paramedic to Change Her Life

CHAPTER ONE

CLAIRE CAMPBELL LET out her breath in a long, contented sigh.

Walking away from her old life and coming to this isolated country on the opposite side of the globe had most definitely been the best decision she'd ever made in her life.

August might be the last month of winter in the southern hemisphere but it felt far more like spring with this small town's hospital garden a glowing swathe of bright yellows and oranges with hundreds of daffodils already in full bloom.

If she wasn't still holding the mug of coffee she'd brought outside with her, having decided to get a breath of fresh air on her break, Claire would have been tempted to throw her arms out sideways and do a three-hundred-and-sixty-degree twirl to embrace this new patch of the planet she'd discovered. Being well up one of Kaikōura's hills meant that she had the best of both worlds as far as the extraordinary views this coastal town could provide. The sea was a glorious stretch of an almost turquoise blue and, behind her, the southern Alps still had an impressive coating of snow on their peaks.

A puff of wind made goosebumps come up on her arms, though. Okay...maybe there was still a hint of winter in the air. She was reminded of her first day in town, only a week or so ago, when ominously dark clouds had unleashed a very unpleasant amount of rain as she tried to find the address of the rental property she'd organised online from the UK.

Claire turned to go back inside but, just as the path curved to go around the corner to where the general practice clinic was attached to one end of the small hospital, she came to a sudden halt. She could hear voices coming from one of the rooms of the clinic. A consulting room? No...if it was this close to the hospital wing, it had to be the office of Tom Atkinson—Claire's new boss, who was the consultant physician and director for the hospital and senior GP for the medical centre.

They were angry voices.

The window had to be open for her to be able to hear the voices this clearly. The people could well be standing right beside it, in fact, and if she walked past she would be somewhere she really didn't want to be—in the middle of an altercation her new boss was having with someone. She could be quite sure that Tom would not want the newest member of his staff to overhear a private conversation.

A very private one, by the sound of it.

'I cannot *believe* you've done this, Hanna. I'm... I'm lost for words. I'm...appalled...'

'Someone had to do it.' The woman's voice was defensive. 'You were never going to do it for yourself, were you?'

'Did it not occur to you that there's a very good reason for that?'

'It's been seven years, Dad. Seven *years*... If you don't do it now, you're never going to and... and you'll be sorry when you're old and lonely.'

'I'm not lonely. And even if I was, what on earth makes you think I'd want to do *online dating*?'

'It's how you find people these days, especially when you live in a town that's not big enough to even have traffic lights. Stop being such a *dinosaur*. Look...it's only been live since this morning and you've been sent fourteen kisses already. All you have to do is click on them and you can send a message back and start getting to know someone.'

'Oh, my God...' The words were slightly muffled, as if Tom might have put his head in his hands. Then they sharpened. 'You haven't put my name on that site, have you?'

Claire knew she shouldn't be listening to this.

She had turned, knowing that she could take the long way round to get to the main doors of the medical centre, and she was poised to move. It was just that her feet were not cooperating quite yet.

She had to admit she was fascinated. She'd noticed that Tom was wearing a wedding ring when she'd finally met him in person last week. Why on earth had his daughter signed him up for online dating? And what had happened seven years ago? Had his wife—Hanna's mother—deserted them? Or died? That was more likely, wasn't it. She might have only just met him but she could be quite sure that Tom was not the kind of man any woman in her right mind would walk away from.

'I haven't even put your photograph on it yet. I used an avatar.'

'Show me.' The words were an icy command. 'What's the name of the site?'

'Ahh...' This Hanna sounded a bit embarrassed now. '*Find The One.*'

The short silence suggested that Tom was tapping and then scrolling on a computer screen. The sound he made to break the silence was a groan.

'You've *got* to be kidding... *That's* my username? *TrustMeI'maDoctor*?'

'I thought it was good.' Hanna sounded like she might be about to burst into tears. 'I'm sorry,

Dad...' Yes, she was sobbing now. 'Please don't be angry with me...'

Her choked words faded as Claire finally began walking briskly back the way she'd come.

'I was only trying to help... I'll take it down...'

It was just as well Tom, along with his colleagues, had to get on with a busy afternoon surgery. There was no time to dwell on the mischief his daughter had been up to. Hopefully, by the time he got home, she would have already deleted his embarrassing profile on that dating site and no harm would have been done. The argument, and the undercurrents, could be pushed back under the carpet where they belonged. With a bit of luck, it would be another seven years before they emerged again.

And, in the meantime, he could tap into the space that made it so much easier to deal with anything that was emotionally disturbing on a personal level. He could simply let it be pushed into the background by thinking about other people rather than himself. He'd learned that the pain of even the worst things could fade eventually and thinking about them too much only added to their power. He'd developed a new mantra all those years ago.

It's not all about me...

How good was it that the waiting room was

full of people that made it so much easier to instantly divert his attention from himself. There were several elderly patients, a pregnant woman, a crying baby, two toddlers fighting over a truck from the toybox and others who were probably trying to ignore what was going on around them by perusing magazines or their phones.

His young receptionist, Kaia, was looking a little flustered as she sorted patient notes between taking phone calls and welcoming patients but his new practice nurse, Claire, seemed admirably calm. She was helping Edward Bramley to negotiate the toddlers with his walking frame, no doubt heading for the nurse's room where she would take Edward's vital signs and a blood test before he came in for his routine appointment to monitor a myriad of health issues he'd collected in his ninety-three years of being alive. Tom could feel her gaze on him as he headed to the desk to collect the pile of case notes Kaia had ready but when he turned to smile at her, she looked away so quickly it made her smooth, shoulder-length bob of silver-grey hair swing. It almost felt as if she was avoiding eye contact with him.

Which was ridiculous. Claire was old enough to be Kaia's grandmother and she hadn't seemed at all shy or retiring in the short time he'd known her so far. Quite the opposite. She was confident, friendly and adventurous. Good grief…she was in her early sixties, a time when most people might be starting to think about slowing down and enjoying a life they'd spent decades building, but Claire Campbell had set off on an adventure to start a whole new life in a foreign country. She also seemed to be very good at her job as a general practice and community nurse, a quick learner for finding her way around a new environment and getting up to speed with different protocols, with decades of experience and common sense to draw on. Exactly the person he'd been searching for to join the staff here at the Seaview Hospital and Medical Centre.

Tom picked up the first set of notes in the basket with his name on it. Through the window of the waiting room, he could see his daughter Hanna walking away from the building. Striding, in fact, as if *she* was the one who had the right to be upset.

And maybe she did. Maybe this really *wasn't* about him?

Hanna had driven a very long way so that she could have a few days with him while she was on study leave and, after overhearing part of a phone call she'd made yesterday, he knew that she was missing a close friend's birthday party in Dunedin. She was a young adult now and she had her own life to live but she'd been thinking about him when she'd decided to set up that profile on a dating site. Had she been fretting, perhaps, that he was lonely now that she'd left home to go to university?

With an inward sigh, Tom firmly pushed his personal life aside. He found a genuine smile as he looked for a familiar face amongst the waiting patients.

'Olivia? Come on through…'

The young woman with long blonde hair stood up. So did the small girl beside her, slipping a hand into her mother's as they followed Tom to the waiting room. Lucy, who was three years old, went straight to the toybox in the consulting room. Olivia sat down in the chair in front of the desk.

'It's lovely to see you, Liv. How can I help today?' He glanced towards Lucy, who didn't look at all unwell. She was stroking the mane and tail of a small plastic unicorn she'd found in the box.

'It's probably nothing,' Olivia said with an apologetic smile. 'But Sam said I had to come and see you. I've…well…it's weird but I've fallen over a few times recently.'

'You've tripped?'

'No. It just seems to happen.'

'Have you injured yourself?'

'I had a sore wrist for a few days but that's

okay now. Except…my arms get really tired when I brush my hair. And maybe it's just that Lucy's getting heavier but it's getting harder to pick her up.'

Tom's eyes narrowed a little as he focused on his patient. He'd known Olivia virtually all her life. He'd come back to work here for the two years of his advanced GP training and she'd been one of his first patients.

'You won't remember this,' he said, 'but you were one of my first patients here. You were a bit older than Lucy and you'd come in for your vaccinations.'

'I do remember. You gave me a lollipop.'

Tom laughed. 'Imagine the outrage if we were seen to be contributing to poor dental health these days?' His smile faded. 'The last time I saw you was for your repeat prescription for your reflux medications. Are those symptoms causing you any more issues?'

Olivia shrugged. 'They're a bit worse, I guess. I'm taking more antacids as well as the pills. It would be good to get the hernia fixed but there's no point if it's going to just come back when I get pregnant again.' Her smile was shy. 'We're trying for a second baby. Sam said that was another reason for me to come and see you—to make sure I'm a hundred percent.'

'He's quite right. Come and jump on the bed for a minute and let me give you a quick check.'

Tom was quick but thorough. He asked questions about any changes to diet or lifestyle as he did his physical examination. He found Olivia's heart rate, blood pressure and temperature were normal. So was his percussion of her chest and her breath sounds. Palpation of her abdomen revealed some epigastric discomfort.

'On a scale of one to ten with one being no pain and ten being the worst you can imagine, what score would you give this abdominal pain?'

'Maybe a four or five? But only when you push on it. Or if I've eaten too much.'

'Okay...lift your leg for me.' He put gentle pressure on her ankle. 'Try and keep it up.'

Tom did find a noticeable weakness in both her arms and legs, however, which was a concern.

'Watch my finger,' he instructed, as he concluded the brief neurological check. 'Keep watching it.' He moved his finger to the right and left, up and down. The ocular muscles were also weak and Tom's level of concern was rising. Despite how well Olivia was looking, instinct was telling him that these could be the first signs of something serious. He really hoped he was wrong.

'I'm going to get you to see our new practice nurse and get some blood tests taken before you leave,' he said, as Olivia got off the bed and straightened her clothes. 'Have you got time?'

'Sure. We're just heading home again after this.' Olivia sat down again. 'Mum said the new nurse went to see Gran to change the dressings on her ulcers the other day and Gran really liked her. She said she was very kind and it didn't hurt as much as usual.'

'Good to hear,' Tom said. 'Her name's Claire and she's come over from England to live in New Zealand for a while. I think she's going to be a real asset to the team.' He was tapping his computer keyboard as he spoke and request forms for the blood tests were starting to emerge from the printer. 'I'd also like to refer you back to the specialist you saw in Christchurch for the hernia. She might want to do a gastroscopy rather than just the barium swallow test you had initially.'

Olivia was helping Lucy put the toys back into the box. 'Okay. That'll be fun, won't it, Lucy? We could go to the big playground while we're there. We might take Daddy with us if he can get a day off work and have a family fun day.'

'Can we get burgers, Mummy? And fries?'

Oliver shared a smile with Tom. 'It makes life easier to live in a place that's too small to have any fast-food outlets.' She led Lucy to the door but then looked over her shoulder with a smile. 'It's a shame about the lollipops though.'

Tom thought so, too. 'I might look into sourcing some sugar-free ones,' he said.

'Now you're talking...' Olivia was still smiling as she left.

The rest of the afternoon clinic passed swiftly, with examinations and prescriptions given for a chest infection that was exacerbating respiratory issues, Edward's slowly increasing level of heart failure, a sprained ankle, different medication for someone whose high blood pressure wasn't responding to current treatment, a new diagnosis of atrial fibrillation and two toddlers, one with an ear infection and the other with an impressively snotty nose and a cough. His final patient was a girl that Hanna had gone to school with who wanted to start using contraception because she and her boyfriend had decided to take their relationship to the next level. Tom gave her a pamphlet.

'There are lots of options, Sasha. Condoms, both internal and external, different types of pills, injections, intra-uterine devices and implants. It can be a lot to take in all at once and there are more things to consider than simply not getting pregnant.'

'Yeah... I know. Like STIs.'

'And whether or not the options have side-effects or risks or use hormones which can affect your periods. Have a read, maybe talk to your boyfriend about it and come back to have a chat with me and we'll get you sorted. You can go and see our practice nurse as well, if there are things you'd rather talk about with her.' His smile was sympathetic. 'It's one of the downsides of living in a small town, isn't it, when your doctor's known you all your life and you're likely to meet him in the supermarket?'

Sasha laughed. 'Everybody knows you're a vault, Dr Atkinson. But yeah…it's a bit weird talking to you about anything to do with sex.'

Tom spent a few minutes typing a summary of the visit into Sasha's digital notes but he found he was thinking just as much about his own daughter. As far as he knew, Hanna did not have a steady boyfriend, but it would be unusual if, as a nineteen-year-old, she did not have a sex life. Was that another reason, on top of assuming he was lonely, why she was suddenly more interested in her father's longstanding lack of female companionship?

Not that it would excuse her misguided decision to put him onto that dating site without his knowledge. Tom's initial shock might have worn off and he knew that Hanna had probably had the best of intentions when she'd put her plan into action, but he still was a long way from being happy. He suspected Hanna felt the same way so it might be a good idea to give things more time to cool down before he went home. She would, hopefully, have distracted herself by focusing on studying for her final exams and he wouldn't want to interrupt that. He had plenty to do here, with a ward round of the inpatients in the hospital and making sure he was up-to-date with any new test results or referral notes that had arrived this afternoon.

It would be nice to be able to look forward to going home, however. Perhaps he could offer some kind of truce so that they could patch up their disagreement more easily?

He flicked her a text.

Be home by seven. I'll pick up some fish and chips for dinner.

He added a lip-licking emoji. There might not be any of the big chain, fast-food restaurants in town but this takeaway meal had been a Friday night treat for Tom and Hanna for many years. Eaten sitting outside in summer on the lawn or maybe down on the beach or on the rug in front of the fire in winter—always straight off the paper, with a puddle of tomato sauce near the chips. A time for just the two of them.

He knew that Hanna would be able to read the hidden message in this offer.

I still love you...

* * *

The practice nurse's room, which was also the medical centre's treatment room, at the end of the corridor leading away from the reception area was becoming a familiar space for Claire.

She knew where all the different vaccines were stored in the fridge, the cupboard that held the urine test dipsticks and the jars for specimen collection and could find any kind of dressings, disinfectant or bandages instantly. She could remove stitches or assist one of the doctors to insert them, take blood samples or chase up results. She had everything she needed to test blood glucose levels, take a blood pressure or do a twelve-lead ECG. It was her job to alert the doctors to abnormal results to see if another appointment needed to be made or to send a text message to the patient to reassure them that nothing abnormal had been found on a blood test, biopsy or scan. She also needed to be available at any time if she was needed as part of a response to an emergency like a cardiac arrest or a local accident.

Claire loved the variety her job offered. The community visits that took her out in the mornings to housebound patients in town or on farms were even more of a bonus in what had to be one of the most spectacular places she could have dreamed of ending up in.

Not that she had ever dreamed about it, mind

you. It had taken a catastrophic implosion of the comfortable, if a little unfulfilling, life she'd been living just outside of London to shake her world up to this extent but she was finally at the point where anxiety about whether she was doing the right thing was being buried by the volume of sheer gratitude that she'd been forced into making such a dramatic change.

The cute little cottage she'd rented for the next six months was also a delight but she wasn't in too much of a hurry to get home. Maybe she should just double check that she hadn't missed any results that might have come in while she'd been so busy in the last couple of hours.

Booting up the computer in her room, Claire remembered the altercation she'd overheard earlier this afternoon between Tom Atkinson and his daughter. What was the name of that online dating site again?

Ah…yes… *Find The One*. Not particularly original. Claire's lips twitched. Neither was *TrustMeI'maDoctor*.

Claire was mystified. Having noticed the ring, she'd assumed that her new boss was married when she'd met him and why wouldn't he be? He was a good-looking middle-aged man who gave the impression of being very happy in his work and his life. An exceptionally good-looking man, in fact. Had he really been single for seven years?

She could hear the echo of a snippet of that conversation.

Someone had to do it... You were never going to do it for yourself, were you?

Okay...that did it.

She could no longer resist doing an internet search for both the dating site and the profile for Tom Atkinson—if it hadn't been taken down already.

It hadn't.

Claire found herself smiling as she discovered that Hanna had chosen a superhero avatar for her father. Cute...

The profile gave a bare minimum of information.

Gender: male
Looking for: female
Age: 54
Marital status: widowed
Location: South Island

Claire blinked. So his wife *had* died. Presumably seven years ago. But he was still wearing his wedding ring? Why...? Had he been so in love with his wife that he couldn't bear to take it off? Or go dating again? No wonder he'd been so horrified by what Hanna had done on his behalf.

But it was kind of cute that she'd done it. She'd

kept his description short but attention-grabbing as well.

Small town guy with a big heart who saves lives for a day job and goes scuba diving for fun. Be nice to have someone's hand to hold for a walk on the beach.

Send a kiss, the site invited its members, with a red heart button to click. *Get one back and you can start talking to the person who might just be 'The One'.*

Tom might have had fourteen kisses a few hours ago but there were twenty-six of them now. Each one came with a thumbnail profile picture to click on. Claire hovered the cursor over one of the pictures—a woman with a wild mane of peroxide blonde hair who seemed to be wearing only underwear—but something stopped her clicking.

Perhaps it was the feeling that she was being watched…

Her head turned so fast she felt something crack in her neck.

How on earth had she not heard someone coming into the room?

Someone who was now staring at the screen of the computer, where it was so very obvious that she wasn't doing anything remotely work-related. She was, in fact, snooping on the private life of one of her new colleagues.

Claire froze. It was possible that she'd never felt quite this mortified in her entire life.

Because this person was none other than the colleague in question, the only person, in fact, who could know who she was snooping on.

It was Tom Atkinson himself.

CHAPTER TWO

TALK ABOUT AWKWARD!

How on earth did the newest member of the staff of this medical centre know that he was enrolled on an online dating site?

Or was this simply a coincidence?

Maybe she'd joined up herself, which might make sense, being in a new town and a new country and wanting to meet people.

Except... Tom suddenly remembered the way Claire had apparently avoided eye contact with him in the waiting room earlier this afternoon. And she was looking...well, as guilty as if she'd been caught with her hand in the proverbial cookie jar. The cursor zipped across the screen to find the X that she clicked on to shut down the website.

'I'm so sorry,' she said. 'I should know better. I *do* know better but...' A corner of her mouth twitched. 'I couldn't help myself.'

'How did you find out about it?' Tom had the horrible thought that maybe he was the last person to know. Was he going to go to the fish and chip shop this evening and find everybody in the queue giving him knowing glances? The 'wink, wink' kind?

'I'd gone outside for a breath of fresh air and the window to your office was open,' Claire said. 'I didn't want you to know I'd overheard any part of what was obviously a private conversation, but by the time I'd realised I could turn around and go the long way back, it was too late. I knew what your username was and...' Her gaze slid sideways to the computer screen. 'I got curious.' She looked up at him. 'I'm really sorry...'

She was. Tom could see the apology in her eyes. Brown eyes, he noticed, but not a really dark brown. More like a dark hazel. His gaze only held hers for a split second but he still managed to catch a glimpse of something other than the colour or a genuine apology in her eyes. There was a spark of...what was it...interest? Mischief, even?

Perhaps there was more to this older, reliable and apparently very competent new staff member than he'd realised. It seemed to be his turn to feel curious.

She seemed to be finding this amusing rather than embarrassing, judging by the way she was biting her lip now, trying not to smile. 'It's certainly attracting a lot of attention.'

'She said she was taking it down.'

'It can take a while,' Claire said. 'Or so I've heard,' she added hastily. 'I've never put a profile up on a dating site, personally.'

'*I* didn't put this one up,' Tom said. 'In case you missed overhearing that part of the conversation. It was my daughter, Hanna, who did that.'

Claire nodded. 'It seems that it's becoming a normal way for young people to meet others these days.'

'I don't want to meet people,' Tom growled. 'And I certainly don't want to *date* anybody.'

Claire actually appeared to shudder at the thought. 'You and me both,' she said. 'Couldn't think of anything I'd like less, to be honest.'

Tom blinked. Why was she so vehement about it? He'd had enough experience with people to know that there had to be a story behind a reaction like that and he suddenly realised how little he knew about his new staff member, other than her age, professional qualifications and how impressed her referees had been.

He cleared his throat. He was relieved that this escapade of Hanna's might not be common knowledge. Perhaps the best way to bury the subject was to simply ignore it and move on.

'How are you settling in here?' he asked. 'I'm hearing good things about you.'

'Really? I've only been here for a week.'

'I had a visit from Olivia Jamieson. You did a house visit to her grandmother to dress her ulcers. She really liked you.'

'I liked her, too. What a character! I can't believe she's nearly a hundred years old and still living in her own home. Nasty diabetic ulcers, though.'

'Don't spread it around, but…' Tom lowered his voice as though he was about to impart something very confidential. 'She said the dressing change didn't hurt as much as it usually did.'

Claire's smile grew until it could only be described as a beam. It lit up her face and even the air surrounding her. 'I love this job. I love the people I'm meeting and I love my wee house and…oh, my goodness—the scenery is extraordinary. I can't wait to get out on a boat and go whale watching.'

'Sometimes,' Tom told her, 'you don't even need to go out on a boat because the whales come in so close. There's a massive submarine canyon that's less than a kilometre from the shore in places. I saw some Southern right whales once, down by the tavern on the esplanade. We ended up with a huge crowd on the beach and the people sitting in the windows of the bar having a glass of wine that day certainly got a bonus.'

'Oh, wow!' Claire seemed thoroughly distracted. 'How amazing would that have been?

I've been wanting to go into that bar and see what's it like,' she added, ducking her head. 'It's just not something I do...you know? I'm not brave enough to go somewhere for a drink by myself.'

'But you're brave enough to go to the other side of the world for a new job?' Tom laughed but then shook his head. 'We should have welcomed you properly by arranging something there.' He looked at his watch. 'I don't have to be home for a while yet. Why don't I see how many of the troops I can round up and we'll go right now.'

The way Claire wrinkled her nose was something he might have expected Hanna to do, not a mature woman, but it was kind of cute.

'It's a bit short notice. And late in the day. Anyone who's still here is likely to be on call, aren't they?'

'True. You should be heading home yourself.' He turned to leave but then turned back. 'Don't you live down that way? Off the esplanade?'

'I do.'

'Why don't I walk down with you and we could have a glass of wine and keep an eye out for a whale or two. To be honest, I could do with winding down a bit more before I get home. I was a bit...annoyed with Hanna about...' he took a furtive glance over his shoulder—there was no one else in the treatment room but he lowered his voice again anyway '...the dating site thing.'

Claire caught her bottom lip between her teeth for a moment. 'I don't blame you,' she said as she released it. 'I would have felt the same way.'

'Have you got a daughter?'

Her expression faltered. 'I did have,' she said. 'She...um...died ten years ago.'

'Oh, God... I'm *so* sorry...' Tom flinched and then groaned. Why hadn't somebody warned him so he wouldn't say something completely insensitive?

'It's okay...you weren't to know. It's not something I put on my CV.' Claire was smiling again, though it looked as if it was more of an effort. 'How 'bout we just rewind anything awkward either of us has said so far and we can start over?'

'Deal.' Tom blew out a sigh of relief. 'But I still owe you a glass of wine, by way of apology for putting my foot in my mouth like that.'

Claire was shaking her head but smiling at the same time. 'Maybe it's me who owes you one—*my* apology for the very unprofessional snooping.'

'In that case, let's just resolve the issue right now, along with dissolving any of the awkwardness we've managed to create. We can go and buy a drink for each other.'

Claire laughed. 'Is that the opposite of going Dutch?'

'Could be.' Tom was holding the door open

as Claire picked up her coat. 'But it's friendlier because you're not paying for your own drink.'

Tom ended up paying for both their glasses of white wine, but Claire simply thanked him rather than protesting. They both knew that he had, albeit inadvertently, trodden on ground that was even more personal than someone's sex life and it was important that they reached a space in which there were no obstructions to working well together.

The nautically themed bar and restaurant—Beachcombers—had comfortable chairs near the bar that afforded a view out to sea over the road, past the trunks of trees that lined the stretch of grass leading to the stony beach.

'Do you know what those trees are?' Claire asked as they sat down. 'They look like really overgrown Christmas trees.'

'They're Norfolk Island pines,' Tom told her. 'Planted well over a hundred years ago now. I believe they're closely related to the monkey puzzle trees that are native to South America.'

Claire eyed him over the rim of her glass as she took a sip of an excellent white wine and Tom grinned.

'Sorry... I didn't mean to sound like some kind of tree nerd. I grew up here and you kind of absorb a lot of local knowledge. It would have made Hanna roll her eyes, too.'

'It would take more than that to make me roll my eyes.' Claire returned his smile. 'How old is Hanna?'

'Nineteen. She's finishing her pre-med course in Health Sciences at university in Dunedin. Up here on study leave for a few days before the rest of her final exams. She's hoping to get into medical school next year.'

'Hoping? Is it very competitive?'

Tom nodded. 'But she's working hard and her marks are great, so fingers crossed.'

He was clearly very proud of his daughter but Claire could see it was making him uncomfortable talking about her. They were both too aware of the elephant in the room. She swallowed hard.

'Ten years ago, my daughter Sophia was in her first year of university,' she told him quietly. 'She was living in a residential hall and she caught meningitis but she was told she just had the flu and got sent home from the campus medical centre. Her roommate called an ambulance in the middle of the night, but by the time we got to the hospital she was deeply unconscious. She never woke up.' Claire cleared her throat before she could sink too far into the past and do something embarrassing like burst into tears. 'She wasn't planning on becoming a doctor, though. She had her sights set on being a marine biologist.' She fixed her gaze on the sea view. 'She would have loved Kaikōura.'

Tom was silent for a long moment. 'Lives can change in a heartbeat,' he said quietly. 'My wife, Jill, died when Hanna was only twelve—a time when a girl really needs her mum the most, I think. It's just been the two of us since then.'

Claire couldn't help shifting her gaze to his left hand.

'I know...' Tom grimaced. 'I kept wearing it to start with because I couldn't bear to take it off. And then I kept wearing it because I didn't want anyone to think I was making myself available. I have no desire to put myself back out there. That's why I might have overreacted a bit to what Hanna did.'

'I totally understand,' Claire told him. 'I might have kept wearing my wedding ring except...' She took a deep breath. 'I threw it away. As far as I could. I pulled it off my finger and hurled it into the Thames.'

'Really?' Tom's eyes widened. 'That's rather dramatic.'

'So was finding my husband in bed with his secretary. A woman half his age. In *our* bed. During my sixtieth birthday party, no less.'

Tom opened his mouth to say something but then closed it again, clearly lost for words.

'It's not as bad as it sounds.' Claire shrugged as she broke the silence. 'It wasn't even the first time he'd had an affair. Our marriage had been over long ago, really. Looking back, losing Sophia was probably the real end. We just kept going out of habit. Or maybe it was too hard to find the energy to do something about it. I should thank Richard to some degree, I guess. He made it impossible for me *not* to do something.'

The silence was longer this time.

'Sorry,' Claire said with a grimace. 'That was way too much information, wasn't it? You're the first person I've ever said that to.' She eyed her glass and tried to find a smile. 'How strong is that wine?'

'Don't worry about it,' Tom said. 'I've never told anyone why I've kept wearing my wedding ring either.' He wasn't smiling but his glance was kind. Understanding. 'Sometimes it's easier to say things to people who don't know you very well. Or maybe we just feel comfortable with each other? That wouldn't be a bad thing, would it?'

'Not at all.'

And magically, her embarrassment about over-sharing evaporated. Comfortable was exactly how she was feeling.

'So…here you are,' Tom said. He sounded

comfortable, too. 'On the opposite side of the world, with a totally new life.'

Claire's smile felt real this time. 'My first adventure,' she agreed. 'But definitely not the last. I'm going to make the most of whatever time I've got left and...it's all about me from now on. I'm not going to complicate my life by including anybody else. Does that sound incredibly selfish?'

'It sounds both brilliant and brave.' Tom raised his glass to clink it against Claire's. 'Go you.'

His smile held a note of admiration and it was warm enough to make the corners of his eyes crinkle. Very blue eyes, she noticed for the first time. Dark blue—like the sea here became further out when it was, presumably, too deep to have that turquoise hue. She took a larger swallow of her wine this time.

'So...' Claire raised her eyebrows. 'Scuba diving, huh...?'

'I got into it at high school. My best mate Pete was passionate about it. He runs a dive school now. It's only a hobby for me. I like going out to play with the seals and get a few crayfish.'

'They're like our Cornish lobsters, yes? Or crawfish?'

'Do you like them?'

'I have to confess, I've never actually tasted them.'

'I'll get you one next time I go out. How 'bout you? What are your hobbies, Claire?'

'I have a new hobby,' Claire said decisively. 'Making the most of every adventure that comes my way. And if it doesn't come my way, I'll go out and find it.'

They clinked almost empty glasses this time and then drank the last of their wine.

A young woman had been collecting empty glasses from a nearby table. She paused as she carried the tray past Tom and Claire. 'Can I get you guys another drink?'

'Not for me,' Tom said. 'I'd better get going. I told Hanna I was going to pick up some fish and chips for dinner. Claire—would you like anything else?'

She shook her head. 'No, thank you.'

'This is Kerry,' Tom told her. 'She was Hanna's best friend right through school.'

'BFFs,' Kerry confirmed. 'And you're the new nurse at the medical centre, aren't you? From England?' She grinned at Claire's expression. 'Word gets around,' she said unapologetically.

She picked up their empty glasses. 'Tell Hanna I'll call her tomorrow,' she said to Tom. 'We need to catch up properly before she heads back to uni.'

And then, to Claire's astonishment, Kerry winked at Tom and lowered her voice to a stage whisper. 'She's going to be thrilled that you're out on a date. Last I heard, she was going to surprise you by putting your profile up on *Find The One*. Now she won't have to.'

She grinned at Claire as she turned to head back to the bar. 'Welcome to Kaikōura,' she said. 'I'm sure you're going to be very happy here.'

Tom was more than lost for words as Kerry headed back to the bar. Claire was almost certain that the poor man was blushing. He wasn't making any move to go and order dinner either.

He made a sound like a stifled groan.

'Looks like I need to apologise again,' he said. 'You must be starting to wonder what you've been dragged into.'

'It's not a problem,' Claire assured him. 'I'm kind of liking the village feel I'm getting here. And I think it's sweet that Hanna doesn't want you to be lonely.'

'I guess. But I don't want her worrying about me. It's hard enough coping with university and living away from home for the first time. I'm the one who's supposed to worry about her, not the other way round.'

He made a kind of growling sound this time. 'I'm going to make sure she's deleted that membership as soon as I get home. And that it never happens again.' He glanced over his shoulder. 'Want me to go and let Kerry know that this is definitely *not* a date? It might be halfway around town by now.'

'I'm not bothered,' Claire said. '*We* know it's not a date and that's all that really matters. And—'

Tom's eyebrows rose. 'And *what*?'

'It just occurred to me that if Hanna does think you were out on a date, she'll be more than happy to delete your profile. She might even stop worrying about you.'

'You wouldn't mind people thinking that we're going out with each other?' He cleared his throat. '*Dating…?*'

'Don't get the wrong idea,' Claire said hurriedly. 'I don't *want* to date anybody. And if I did, it wouldn't be my new boss. But if it's the solution to your…um…personal issue that I accidentally managed to get involved in today, I'm quite happy to go along with people *thinking* that we might be dating.'

Tom was staring at her. 'It might work both ways,' he said slowly.

'How?'

'A new, unattached and attractive woman in town is not going to go unnoticed in a small place like this. If it gets around that *we're* getting to know each other, nobody's going to hit on you.'

A silence fell between them that stretched on.

And on.

Or maybe it was just Claire's attention had caught so completely on something Tom had said that she wasn't hearing anything else.

He thought she was *attractive*?

Yep. He was still talking.

'...so we could both adopt a "neither confirm nor deny" policy and we'd be the only ones who knew the truth. But it's not as though we'd be doing something dishonest and... I don't know about you, but I'd be more than happy to spend some more time in your company.'

There was no hint of anything more than friendliness in either Tom's tone or expression. If he considered her to be attractive it was purely an impersonal observation. She had, after all, considered him to be an exceptionally good-looking man, hadn't she?

And she was on a side of the world where she didn't know a soul. It would be stupid to find reasons to not make a friend.

So she smiled at Tom.

'Same,' she said.

'Ooh... Fish and chips? It's not even Friday.'

'I felt too lazy to cook.' These days, they tended to eat at the kitchen table rather than lounging on the floor or the lawn. Tom unfolded the white newsprint paper as Hanna got the bottle of tomato sauce from the fridge.

'How's the study going?'

'Good. I need to do a practice multi-choice test for microbiology on genes, inheritance and selection next. Want to help? You could ask me the questions and explain anything I get wrong.'

'I might have forgotten a lot of that stuff.'

'Doubt it.' Hanna leaned past Tom to squirt the sauce into a puddle on a corner of the paper. 'What sort of fish is it?'

'Tarakihi. We got lucky—it was fresh in today.'

They both knew this flaky white fish was Hanna's favourite. She caught her father's glance.

'I'm sorry, Dad...about...the dating site thing. I've deleted your profile but it might take a day or two to disappear.'

'Okay. Thanks...'

Hanna sat down, picked up a piece of battered fish and broke it in half to release fragrant steam. 'Sounds like you don't need it anyway.'

'Oh?' Tom had turned back to the kitchen bench to rip off some paper towels to use as serviettes. He knew exactly what Hanna was referring to but it was easy to play dumb.

'Yeah... Kerry sent me a pic of you having a drink at the Beachcombers. Who was your date?'

Tom opened his mouth to deny that it had been a date but stopped himself just in time. Neither confirm nor deny, he reminded himself. This was it. The moment where he would find out whether

Hanna would stop worrying about him. If she could focus on enjoying her own life and not feel any need to interfere with his.

'I was with Claire Campbell.' He kept his tone casual. 'Our new practice nurse.'

'The English lady?'

'Yes.'

'So she's single then? She's quite attractive, isn't she?'

Tom remembered telling Claire she would be seen as an unattached and attractive new woman in town and…yes…that shiny, silvery hair and her soft brown eyes *were* a very nice combination. The way her face could light up with that eye-catching smile was more appealing, however. So was her attitude to life.

Claire had been through a personal loss in life as crushing as his own but her response—now, at least—was very different to his own. Tom had made his life smaller. He had focused on his daughter and his work and, apart from his hobby of scuba diving, he'd deliberately shut other pleasures out of his life. Like companionship. And sex. Anything that had the risk of emotional complications or, worse, loss associated with it, in fact. His mantra had been that it wasn't all about himself because putting someone else first made it easier to protect himself from risk.

Claire's new mantra was that it was *all* about

herself and she intended to make the most of the rest of her life. She was out to have fun. Adventures.

Adventurous people were always interesting.

If they had to spend some time in each other's company now and then to keep up the smokescreen that would prevent Hanna worrying about his personal life, it wasn't going to be a hardship. Maybe it wouldn't hurt if a bit of her attitude to life rubbed off on him. He was probably overdue for a bit of fun himself.

He'd almost forgotten what Hanna's question had been.

'Yes,' he said aloud. 'She's definitely single and she *is* a very attractive woman but she's only just arrived in the country a week or so ago.' Tom reached for one of the crispy battered fish fillets. 'Don't you or Kerry go starting any rumours. Give the poor woman a chance to get settled in.'

'Don't worry... I get it.' Hanna tilted her head. 'It's early days... We'll make sure we don't scare her off.'

She probably thought her smile was hidden as she ate another chip but Tom could almost feel her breathing a sigh of relief and see a thought bubble forming over her head.

My work is done...

CHAPTER THREE

'Claire, can I get you to give me a hand, please?'

'Of course.' Claire was only too happy to help. It had, in fact, made her happy just to see Tom appear in the doorway of the treatment room. 'I was just about to start sending test result text messages but they can wait.' She got to her feet as Tom stood back from the open door.

'Come on in, Carl. Claire's not going to bite.'

A man with curly grey hair and grizzled stubble on his face entered the room. He was wearing an oilskin vest over a heavy knitted jumper with one sleeve pulled up. What looked like an oily rag was wrapped around his hand. His attempt at a smile was enough of a failure to let Claire know he was in severe pain.

'Let me help you,' she said, going towards him. She caught Tom's gaze. 'Bed or chair?'

'Bed,' Tom said. 'Carl might look as tough as old boots but he's just the kind to faint at the sight of a needle.'

'Yeah…right…' Carl gave a dismissive huff.

He evaded any help from Claire as he climbed onto the bed and lay back against the pillows, the rag-wrapped hand being held protectively by the wrist at head height.

'Carl is one of the favourite boat skippers in town,' Tom told her. 'He does dive trips and whale watching tours. He's managed to get a finger caught in a pulley this morning, though, and he's done a good job of squashing it. Might well lose the tip. Could be lucky to keep the rest of it.'

Claire lifted her eyebrows. Tom gave a single shake of his head.

'Not the kind of minor surgery we can do. I've called for an ambulance to transfer him to Christchurch but I want to get a ring block in to deal with the pain and clean things up a bit. That rag from the boat is not going to cut it as a sterile dressing. When did you last have a tetanus booster, Carl?'

'No idea.'

'I'll check your notes but I'm pretty sure you're going to need a top-up.'

Claire was opening cupboards to grab supplies as Tom went to the basin to scrub his hands. She'd had another week or so to get to know where everything was in this room so she could work more swiftly now. She put alcohol wipes, syringes, needles and local anaesthetic into a kidney dish that she put on a trolley. She also collected disinfectant, dressings and bandages. Finally, she pulled a couple of plastic-backed sterile sheets from a box like an oversized packet of tissues. By the time Tom was drying his hands and then reaching to pull gloves from the box on the wall, she had the trolley positioned beside the bed and was pulling on gloves herself.

She'd also had another week or so to get used to working with Tom in the wake of their agreement to let Hanna think he didn't need any assistance in his love life. The extra time had confirmed how good he was at his job, how respected and valued he was in this close-knit community, but it had also become apparent that Hanna wasn't the only one who believed the pretence that there might be something simmering between herself and Tom. So far it had been easy to stick to the 'neither confirm nor deny' tactic and nobody pushed her when she simply smiled and said how much she was enjoying working with everybody at the medical centre and how lovely it was to be making new friends.

That hadn't stopped a few envious glances coming her way from other women, mind you, which was understandable. She slid a sideways glance at Tom, who had picked up an ampoule of lidocaine and was starting to draw the drug up into a syringe. He *was* a very attractive man. Even better, he was a very *nice* man.

'If you can get rid of the rag, it would be helpful,' he said to Claire. Then he smiled at Carl. 'We'll have you sorted in no time, mate.'

'Sorry...' Claire apologised in advance. 'I know it hurts to move your hand. I'm going to put one of these waterproof sheets on the bed beside you here, and if you can hold your hand over it, I'll take the cloth off before you put your hand down.'

Carl's hands had oil ingrained into the skin and under his nails. Claire carefully unwrapped the cloth to reveal the badly squashed ring finger on his left hand.

'Put the hand palm down,' Tom instructed Claire. 'I'll get you to hold the wrist and help keep his hand steady, please.'

Tom ripped open a small foil package to remove an alcohol wipe and swab the area around the base of the finger.

'We have to do something about that wedding ring,' he noted. 'It's almost disappeared under the swelling already. We'll cut it off once we've numbed your finger, Carl.'

'The missus won't be too happy about that.' Carl was staring up at the ceiling, clearly not wanting to see how bad the finger injury was.

'Can't be helped,' Tom said. 'And it needs to come off as soon as possible before that finger gets any more swollen or I won't be able to use my ring cutter.'

'You'll be able to get the ring fixed,' Claire assured him.

'Might keep it as a souvenir,' Carl muttered. 'In case I don't get to keep my finger.'

Tom was about to inject into the web on each side of the finger where it joined the palm. A quick glance was a silent query as to whether Claire was ready to counteract any movement from Carl during what was going to be the most painful part of this procedure. She settled her hands across his forearm and wrist and tried to think of something to distract him.

'I'm really looking forward to doing a whale watch boat trip, myself,' she said. 'What's the name of your boat so I'll know who to book with?'

'*Time and Tide.*'

'As in you don't wait for anybody?'

'More like make the most of today.' Carl winced as the needle went into his hand,

'I like that philosophy,' Claire told him as she tightened her grip on his arm a little. 'I'm guessing a really calm day is best?'

Carl's voice was strained. He could feel the anaesthetic being injected. 'You wouldn't believe how many people get sick out there. Especially on a smaller boat like mine. It's a catamaran. Sits nice and low in the water so you're closer to the action and I only take out about ten people at a time. Twelve, max.' He was still gritting his teeth as Tom inserted the needle for a second time on the other side of his finger.

'What sort of whales might I get to see?' Claire asked. 'Tom told me he saw some really close to the shore—what were they? Southern something?'

'Southern right,' Tom said. 'But giant sperm whales are the stars of the show, aren't they, Carl?'

'My favourites are the humpbacks,' Carl said. 'They can really put on a show, if you're lucky.' He let his breath out in a sigh which suggested that he was already noticing a difference in his pain level. He opened his eyes to look at Claire. 'How 'bout I keep an eye on the weather and give you a heads-up whenever it's looking good. Should coincide with a day off for you, eventually.'

'That would be great. Thank you!'

'Not sure when I'll be back on deck, mind you. Ooh...that's feeling a lot better, Doc. Pain's almost gone.'

'It can take up to ten minutes for the full effect and it should last long enough to get you to specialist care in the big smoke. Don't move. Can you find the ring cutter for me, please, Claire? It should be on the bottom shelf of the cupboard in the far corner—it's a black plastic box about the size of a laryngoscope kit. Should be labelled.'

Claire hadn't seen the specialist tool that Tom got out of the case. He inserted a thin, flat metal plate under the ring on Carl's finger.

'Protection,' he said. 'So I don't go too far and cut more than the ring.'

Carl shook his head. 'Hope you know what you're doing, Doc.'

Tom grinned. 'I don't get to play with this toy very often but I have done it before. Claire, can you get a syringe and fill it with saline? The metal gets hot so it'll be useful to cool it off occasionally.'

It took time to use the battery-powered disc cutter and then a tiny pair of spreaders that opened the ring far enough to remove. It left a deep mark between a normal-looking hand and a finger that had ballooned into a large sausage shape.

'Flush the wound as best you can, Claire, and then we'll dress the finger and splint the hand. I'm going to check Carl's notes and get a tetanus booster sorted.'

Claire cleaned and dressed the finger and then bandaged the whole hand into a splint. She was tying the knot of a sling behind Carl's neck as Tom came back in. 'Our ambulance will be here in a minute,' he said. 'Just time to give you that booster. They'll take you halfway and a crew from Christchurch will take over.'

Minutes later and Carl was walking out to the ambulance.

'I'll get a report from the specialists,' Tom said. 'But come and see me when you get back if you're worried about anything.'

'Will do.'

'I'll look forward to hearing from you, too,' Claire told Carl. 'I'm going to wait for my whale watching until you are back on deck.'

Tom followed Claire back into the clinic.

'Is there something else you need?' she asked. 'Aren't you due to do a ward round?'

Tom wasn't really surprised that Claire was obviously becoming as familiar with his routine as she was with all aspects of her own job. She was, hands down, the best practice nurse he'd ever worked with.

'I am, yes...but I'm hoping I'm going to find an urgent appointment's been made by the gastroenterology department in Christchurch for Olivia Jamieson. If there isn't, I might need to chase my referral up. I would really prefer her to be seen as soon as possible.'

'I've got the link open on my computer in the

treatment room. Not sure I've seen anything about Olivia, though.'

'I'll come in for a minute and check.'

Tom sat down at the desk tucked in behind the door. He could hear Claire busy dealing with contaminated rubbish like swabs that had to go into the hazards rubbish bag and the sharps like needles that went into the plastic wall container as he scrolled through the clinic email marked for his attention.

'How did Hanna go with her exam yesterday?' Claire asked.

'She's happy. She's got a couple more next week and then she'll start the summer job that she's really excited to have scored.'

'What is it?'

'An entry-level position as a medical laboratory technician. They'll give her on-the-job training.'

'Sounds great. She'll be learning a lot and getting paid for it as well. I hope she'll get some time off, though. You must be missing her.'

'I hear from her most days.' Tom turned away from the screen. He'd have to check again later or try ringing the specialist, although he knew how busy they would be. 'She's been asking about you.'

'Oh...?' Claire had her back to him as she put the kidney dishes into the benchtop steriliser. She sounded...wary?

As well she might. Hanna wanted details of the embryonic relationship she believed he had with Claire.

'She wants an update,' Tom said.

'What kind of update?' Claire looked over her shoulder. 'A full report on an *actual* date?'

'That would work.' Tom got to his feet. He felt slightly uncomfortable at the thought of having anything *like* an actual date with Claire because it made him instantly more aware of her as a woman than as his colleague. She was more than simply attractive he'd decided at some point since Hanna's visit when the plan to let her think he was dating Claire had been hatched. That shiny silvery hair was like moonlight and it made her brown eyes look even darker. Warmer. She looked at least a decade younger than he knew she was. Younger than him, even. Not that he was thinking about her age. Or her attractiveness. He needed to think of a pretend date that he could tell Hanna about.

'It might not be a good look if we're only meeting to have a drink,' he said. 'Maybe we could do something that looks like a healthier kind of date.'

'Such as?'

'A movie? A walk? A visit to the lookout?'

'Ooh… The lookout on the hill where you can see both sides of the peninsula? I haven't been up there yet. I drove up to Blenheim on my last day off.'

'Let's go after work. A quick selfie with the wind in our hair and the view behind us will be more than enough to keep Hanna happy.'

He was feeling rather happy about the prospect himself, in fact. Tom headed for the door. It was definitely time he went and got on with that ward round.

It was only a thirty-minute walk up to the lookout, which should have warmed them up very well but there was an icy wind blowing on the top of the hill that felt like it was coming straight off those snow-capped mountains. They could see over South Bay on one side of the peninsula but the view they needed as a background was in the opposite direction where the ocean swept out to one side and the dramatic peaks of the mountains towered over the township and made the distinctive pointy tips of the Norfolk pines look the size of toothpicks.

'The mountains are called the Seaward Kaikōura Range,' Tom told her. 'But they're really the northernmost section of the Southern Alps that go all the way down to Queenstown in Central Otago. That's another part of the country you need to explore on this adventure you're having.'

'Is Mount Cook part of the Southern Alps? That's the tallest mountain in New Zealand, isn't it?' Claire was trying not to let her teeth chatter. She couldn't feel her cheeks or her nose now but the view was definitely worth it.

'Sure is, even though ten metres fell off it in an earthquake back in the nineties.' Tom didn't seem to be feeling the cold as much as Claire was. He was fishing his phone out of his pocket. 'You any good at taking selfies?'

'I've never taken one in my life,' Claire confessed. 'And I suspect my fingers would be too cold to push the button, anyway.'

'Can't say I've taken many either, but let's see what we can do.'

They turned so that the mountains and ocean would be behind them and Tom held his phone up as far away as he could reach. Only half of their faces were on each edge on the screen.

'We need to be closer.' Tom's arm was pressed against Claire's but then he lifted it and put it around her shoulders.

She instantly felt warmer.

And it felt...nice. How long had it been since she'd had a man's arm around her like this?

'Okay...try and look happy,' Tom instructed. 'This is supposed to be a date, remember?'

Claire could see both their faces in the phone's screen. Tom was grinning, as if he was having the best time. Claire tipped her head a little as she practised a big smile and it ended up against Tom's shoulder as he took the photograph.

'This is great,' he declared. 'But let's do another one just to make sure.'

Claire was getting used to the feeling of Tom's arm and her smile felt way more genuine now. She found herself looking up at Tom rather than at the phone. He seemed taller up this close.

Astonishingly good-looking with the way the wind was whipping his hair into a rough tumble of waves. And that smile...

Oh, my goodness...it was one of the loveliest smiles Claire had ever seen. She'd totally forgotten how cold she'd been feeling only a minute or two ago. Maybe because of the warm glow that her body was suddenly producing?

It was a glow she hadn't experienced in too many years to count, but Claire knew instantly what it was and she found herself moving away from the touch of Tom's body. Being attracted to him was definitely not part of the plan. Being attracted to anyone was not in any plan Claire had in her life going forward. Been there, done that and she didn't even want to wear the tee shirt any longer.

If she just ignored it, would it quietly go away?

Tom didn't seem to have noticed. He was checking out the photos.

'I don't want to blow my own trumpet,' he said, 'but this one's great. Look at that view.'

It *was* a great photo. Good enough for a travel blog with that backdrop of mountains and ocean. What Claire noticed more, however, was that the way she was gazing up at Tom, with her head against his arm, could be seen as blatantly advertising how attracted she was to the man.

How inappropriate was that?

At least Tom would think she'd only been acting for the sake of the staged photo he'd requested so that they could give Hanna the impression that they were on a real date. This was for Hanna's benefit, after all, so that she could stop worrying about her dad and focus on her own life, but it was a win-win situation for everybody involved, wasn't it? Tom could avoid having any interference with the way he wanted to live *his* life. And Claire had her own reasons to be grateful for this unexpected playacting—the protection of declaring herself unavailable for dating with the bonus of having a new friendship in her life. A platonic one that had strong enough boundaries to render it completely safe.

They were doing this because the last thing Tom wanted was to be genuinely dating anyone and Claire was just as keen to avoid becoming romantically involved with anyone again. If she ever changed her mind about that, it certainly wouldn't be happening with a man who was her boss, with the additional risk of making her professional life uncomfortable if it turned to custard. Not only that—Tom was seven years younger than she was, for heaven's sake. Young enough to be her...okay, not her son, of course, but...little brother?

'That photo's the one,' Claire declared. 'It should be more than enough to keep Hanna happy for a while.'

Tom didn't seem so sure. 'Next time,' he said, 'we'll go to the movies. It'll be a whole lot warmer, I promise.'

It was actually far more pleasant than Tom had expected to have a companion to...well, *do* stuff with. Things that his mate, Pete, might have thought it was strange to spend his time off doing. The kind of things that Tom hadn't done since Hanna became old enough to want to hang out with her friends rather than spend too much time in her dad's company.

Things like grabbing last-minute tickets to go to the latest blockbuster being screened in the only movie theatre in town. The selfie he took outside the iconic old pink art deco building got a response from Hanna by way of a text message that consisted of a whole line of heart emojis. It was like getting an A+ on a report card for the project of making Hanna think he was happy enough in his personal life that there was no need for her to interfere.

He could possibly have relaxed his efforts a bit after that but...this was fun. Claire was great company, and they both knew that this was never going to be anything more than a friendship, so it was...

Completely safe. That's what it was. So why not enjoy it?

There was absolutely no danger of it being considered as anything significant. On either side. Claire had only recently escaped a marriage that had clearly been less than ideal and she was embracing the freedom to do whatever she wanted without...how had she put it? Oh, yeah...that she wasn't going to complicate her life by including anybody else.

Tom could understand that. Why would she want to risk getting trapped in another less-than-ideal relationship? Was his aversion to the risk of getting too close to someone even stronger because his marriage *had* been so good? Because he couldn't face the idea of having to pick his life up after having had it completely shattered?

Not that it mattered. They both had very valid reasons for not wanting anything more than a friendship and that was what made this safe enough to embrace.

He took Claire to the most famous of the crayfish caravans that were dotted along the coastline and sold freshly caught crayfish, cooked or still alive if you wanted to do the cooking yourself. That would have been Tom's choice, given that he hadn't had a chance to go diving for a while, until he saw how fast Claire took a backwards step when he held one up to show her. The waving long antennae, too many legs and the claws were obviously way too close for comfort and, while her expression made him have to stifle laughter as he apologised, he made a mental note to be more considerate when he'd caught his own to cook on the barbecue or under the grill for her at his house.

The thought made him blink and he was still thinking about it when they sat at one of the picnic tables beside the caravan to share a freshly cooked crayfish tail served with garlic butter and lemon. Was he really thinking of inviting Claire home for dinner? *Just* Claire?

Maybe he should make it a work thing and invite everybody for a casual get-together?

Nah... Tom lifted another delicious mouthful of the white meat from the bright orange shell of the crayfish tail. It would be harder to keep up the pretence of this being anything more than a friendship if it was out of work hours and they had an audience. He might have to start giving some thought to how this was going to work when Hanna came home for a visit, however. She would be an even sharper-eyed audience than anyone they worked with.

Not that he needed to worry about that yet. He could keep enjoying being alone together with Claire in the meantime.

On another shared day off, they drove even further north to have lunch at a popular café in Kekerengu that had a gift shop full of tempting locally made products. Claire stopped on the way out to admire a blanket that had a pattern of small woolly sheep woven into it.

'That's such a Kiwi blanket,' she said.

The urge to give her something that she might treasure was unexpectedly strong, 'Let me buy it for you,' Tom offered. 'As a thank you gift.'

'What for? You've just taken me out for a lovely lunch. And consider this fair warning that I'm definitely paying next time.'

'I just wanted to say thank you for going along with this... I don't know what to call it...this fake dating? Hanna's so happy about it. I'm totally off the hook for any future online capers.'

Claire went quite still. 'Do you know, I'd almost forgotten about that,' she said. 'It's started to feel like...spending time with a friend. Our friendship isn't fake, is it?'

Tom's smile was fading rapidly. 'Of course not.

I'm enjoying this as much as you are. I'd still like to get the blanket for you, though.'

But Claire shook her head. 'I'm travelling light,' she said. 'Who knows when I'll get itchy feet to set off on my next adventure? I don't want to be accumulating luggage on the way.'

'Fair enough.'

They stopped on the way back to Kaikōura that day to visit the seal colony. A fenced walkway provided the perfect viewing point to get close enough to watch without disturbing the seals. He got his phone out to take pictures of the adults sunbathing like giant brown slugs on top of rocks big enough to keep them safe from being annoyed by the tribe of playful babies that were rock scrambling, sliding over piles of kelp or learning to swim in the rock pools but he ended up taking photos of Claire laughing at their antics.

And they were both laughing in that selfie.

Tom looked at it later, intending to send it to Hanna, but something made him pause. Was it because he was struck by how gorgeous Claire was, with the sunlight caught in her hair making it look like a halo? And that *smile*... He was smiling now, just looking at the image of it. Not as widely as he was smiling in the photograph, however. He hadn't seen himself looking *this* happy in years and, for some peculiar reason, it suddenly made him feel sad enough to bring a lump to his throat.

Why? Because it was reminding him of the companionship and support of a happy marriage and a beloved wife? Underlining what was missing from his life now? Even the pretence of having found someone new was making him happier.

So maybe he needed to think about that. About whether he was finally ready to invite someone else into his life again.

Not Claire, of course. She'd made it very clear that she was only here on a temporary basis. Kaikōura was simply the first stop on the series of adventures she was going to pack into her life. The worst thing he could do would be to fall for someone when it was inevitable that he would lose her in the near future. That would put him back to square one and if that happened Tom knew how unlikely it was that he would ever want to try again.

But could that also be why he was feeling sad looking at this photo? Because it was recording a relationship that could never be anything more than fake?

No. Tom remembered what Claire had asked earlier today.

'Our friendship isn't fake, is it?'

He cleared that lump from his throat. It certainly wasn't. Their friendship was becoming very special. Important. Potentially life-changing, even?

Tom tapped the share button and sent the image to Hanna.

We had a great day today. Hope you did, too.

CHAPTER FOUR

MAYBE THE STARS weren't aligned quite right today.

Claire had felt like something was out of kilter ever since she'd woken up this morning, even though she couldn't think of any good reason to feel this way. It was probably just life, she told herself as she arrived at work to start her community house calls. Some days were simply better than others.

Mabel Jamieson certainly wasn't having a good start to her day, as Claire had to spend more time cleaning the infected ulcers on her feet and the antiseptic solution on what was nothing more than raw flesh had to be excruciatingly painful.

'I'm so sorry, Mabel. We'll get some fresh dressings on very soon and they should stop hurting so much.'

'You just do what you need to do, love. I'm not complaining.'

'You never do.' Claire looked up with a smile

for a patient she had become very fond of in a matter of only weeks. 'You're a legend.'

Mabel shook her head. 'You expect things to go wrong at my age. What's you don't expect is that a darling young one like our Livvy is going to get sick. She had to have all sorts of tests done last week in Christchurch. She said she got put right inside some enormous machine. For a scan.'

'It would have been a CT scan. Or maybe an MRI. Did she say if there were strange noises happening?'

'No. But she had to go back the next morning and they put her to sleep to put a camera down her throat to take a biopsy of something. She did say she was nervous about getting the results. She thinks she might have an ulcer herself, in her gullet, and that's why she gets such bad indigestion. At least I can keep my weight off my feet to give things a chance to heal. She's a busy young mum—she can't stop *eating*, can she?'

'Ulcers *are* treatable,' Claire said, trying to sound reassuring. 'And Olivia might need to avoid certain foods, but she wouldn't need to stop eating completely if that *is* what's causing her problems.' She found a smile for Mabel. 'This infection is starting to respond to the antibiotics, I think. Tom will be happy to hear that.'

Tom had been worried that if things got any worse, Mabel might well need to be admitted to hospital and when you were nearly a hundred years old there was no guarantee that you would get to go home again.

'Sorry,' she said again, as Mabel winced beneath her hands at the sting of the liquid. 'That's the last one.'

Her elderly patient was much happier a few minutes later as Claire began applying the specialised absorbent dressings that were also impregnated with beneficial medications.

'So what's this I hear about you and young Tom Atkinson?' Mabel queried, her tone much brighter. 'Is he courting you?'

'Good heavens, no.' Claire's laugh was genuine. 'What a wonderful old-fashioned expression that is. No,' she repeated, more decisively. 'We're just good friends.'

'I've heard that one before.' Mabel chuckled but didn't pry any further. 'Enjoy yourself,' was all she said. 'Make the most of still being young enough to have that kind of fun.'

Claire pretended to be too busy with securing the dressings to respond but she was smiling. Mabel had reminded her of why the not so good things in life had their purpose—they made you appreciate the really good things even more.

Like the day she'd spent with Tom last weekend and they'd gone halfway to Blenheim to have lunch and then watched the baby seals playing on the way home.

She'd been regretting not buying that sheep blanket, though. Was her decision not to acquire something that she would love to have on her bed, or cuddle up under on the couch, really about not collecting too many possessions for when she moved on?

Or was it because Tom had offered to buy it for her and that felt like a gift that would be too significant?

A gift that might make her start believing things that had no basis in reality? Like how Tom felt about her, for instance. And whether there might be something happening that was more than purely a friendship.

Claire shook the thought off as she put her kit back into the back hatch of the hospital car she used for her community visits and slammed the door shut.

Mabel was old and wise.

She should just enjoy this friendship she'd found with Tom. He'd made it very clear there was nothing more on offer. Heavens above…this had only started because he was so determined to avoid going anywhere near that type of relationship with someone.

And thank goodness for that.

It was the last thing she wanted as well. What

if she repeated the mistake she'd made before and settled for a marriage based on nothing more than friendship? One that seemed good enough because she'd never found something that was as magical as she thought falling in love was supposed to be? It hadn't been good enough, though, had it? Richard's affair with his secretary hadn't been his first but Claire had chosen to ignore her suspicions until it became blatant enough to make that impossible. Had it been that she hadn't tried hard enough not to let grief push them so far apart there was no way back? That she didn't want confirmation that the mediocrity of this marriage was her fault? That *she* wasn't good enough?

She'd certainly been left with that impression after finding him with a woman who was so much younger than herself. So much more attractive. No wonder her husband had fallen so madly in love.

He'd found what she'd never been able to find when she was young enough to believe it could happen.

But to expect a fairytale romance at this stage in her life?

How ridiculous would *that* be?

Tom read the report that had just arrived in his inbox during his lunch break.

He put down the sandwich he'd been about to take a bite of, his appetite gone. He closed his eyes for a long, long moment. And then he opened them and read it again. He looked at the scan images and his heart sank even further.

He picked up the phone.

'Dr Atkinson...hey! Oops...hang on a sec... Lucy, that's only one shoe. You need *two* shoes to go to kindy, darling. Go and find the other one. Sorry...' Olivia sounded a bit breathless now. 'It's always a bit of a rush to get her off to afternoon kindy. Is this about my results?'

'It is. Can you come in this afternoon and I'll go over the test results and scan images and things with you. Maybe while Lucy's at kindy?'

'Um...okay...what sort of time?'

Oh, help...how obvious was it that the news wasn't good when reassurance couldn't be given over the phone? How great would it have been to be able to open this conversation by saying something like 'Look, it's nothing to worry about, but could you come in...'

Lucy calling in the background covered Tom's slight hesitation.

'You find it, Mummy...*now*... I want my *shoe*...'

'How does two o'clock sound?' Tom took a breath, trying to keep his tone upbeat. 'You might like to bring someone with you. Like Sam? Or your mum?'

The silence felt fragile now. As if something, or some*one*, could break at any moment.

'Yeah…okay. I guess Mum's just down the road. She could get away from the shop for a bit.'

'Great. Just tell Kaia when you get to Reception and she'll come and find me.'

It was another busy afternoon clinic in the medical centre.

Claire took blood samples and a urine dipstick test for someone who probably had a urinary tract infection. She took blood pressures for people who needed regular monitoring and administered a vaccination for shingles for someone in their sixties and one for whooping cough for a woman in her fifties who was about to become a grandmother for the first time.

'I'd never forgive myself if I passed something horrible on to the baby,' she told Claire. 'Are there any other vaccinations I should get?'

'The MMR is recommended,' Claire said. 'That's measles, mumps and rubella.'

'I definitely had a measles vaccination when I was a kid.'

'Yes, but immunity fades over time. The pneumonia vaccination is another one that's on the list you might like to consider. I've got a pamphlet I can give you to read.'

She took a twelve-lead ECG that had been scheduled for ninety-three-year-old Edward Bramley.

'I'll give this to Dr Atkinson and he can tell you about it in your appointment,' she told him as she helped him manoeuvre his walking frame through the door of the treatment room. She saw Kaia, further down the corridor, showing Olivia Jamieson and an older woman into Tom's consulting room and she caught her breath. Had the results from the numerous investigations that Mabel had said Olivia had been subjected to finally come in? The older woman was about Claire's age so she assumed that it might be her mother that had come to the appointment with her. Her heart went out to her if it was. What was worse, she wondered—to be without family completely, as she was, or to be sandwiched between trying to support a sick parent and child at the same time?

Oddly, it made her feel very lonely.

Claire was hoping she could catch up with Tom and find out what was happening for Olivia but he was nowhere to be seen whenever she went out to Reception to collect the next person who had an appointment booked with her. She spent one time slot with someone who was taking part in a smoking cessation programme and then she had stitches to remove and a dressing change for Carl the boat skipper, who had ended up only having the tip of his ring finger amputated after the accident with the pulley.

'That's healing really well,' she told him. 'You'll still need to keep it dry a bit longer, though.'

'I'm wearing a rubber glove on the boat. A bright pink one.' He grinned at Claire. 'Get some funny looks from the tourists. When are you going to come out and do some whale watching?'

'As soon as I get some time off that coincides with some good weather. I haven't forgotten, I promise.'

She did forget almost as soon as Carl had gone, however, as her next patient arrived. Even after clinic hours were well over she was still busy, writing up notes for all the appointments she'd done that afternoon and tidying up and restocking the treatment room so that it was ready for any emergency that might come in.

What she hadn't forgotten was that Mabel's granddaughter had been to see Tom, but he wasn't in his consulting room when she went to look for him. She'd send him a text message later, she decided, but when she was walking out of the medical centre's front door to head home for the day she saw him coming out of the hospital wing.

She hadn't been wrong about the stars not being aligned very well today, had she? And someone else had been affected far more than she had. Tom was far enough away to not be able to read his expression clearly but she didn't need to. She could sense that he was carrying a weight on his shoulders that had been caused by a very bad day. What took her completely off-guard was the way that made *her* feel. It was a squeeze on her heart that was hard enough to be physically painful.

Hard enough to be a warning?

The kind of complications that came with caring too much about other people was something Claire had resolved to leave behind in her old life. Tom Atkinson might have enlisted her assistance to pretend that there might be something more than friendship between them but that was all it was. A pretence.

This was taking the sheep blanket disquiet to a whole new level. Friendship was acceptable. Anything more was not. Surely caring about someone else enough to make it feel as if their wellbeing was far more important than her own was stepping into unacceptable territory?

She could already guess that the news about Olivia wasn't good. She hadn't seen any results come through so maybe they'd been emailed directly to Tom, which would suggest that it was something really serious. Would Tom want her poking her nose into his personal feelings about it? They barely knew each other. This was Tom's hometown and Olivia Jamieson was probably one of many patients he'd known for a significant part of their lives. He must have had to deal with countless difficult emotional situations, professional and personal, and many would have been a mix of both, given this small community. He had managed without Claire in the past and he would manage without her in the future when she'd moved on to her next adventure.

She needed her freedom to be able to do that without feeling guilty. Or regretful.

And Tom needed his privacy.

The general practitioners in this small town still made house calls on a regular basis but they weren't usually at this time of the evening when it didn't involve an emergency.

Tom had just made two such visits, the second one because Olivia's mother, Yvonne, had asked if he could be the one to break the news to Mabel that her granddaughter was going to need surgery for something a lot more serious than the hiatus hernia they already knew she had.

The sun was already setting by the time he was heading home but he still parked along the esplanade and got out of his car to go towards the beach. He needed to breathe some of that cool, salty air and listen to the waves tumbling pebbles as they rolled onto the shore for a while. He barely noticed the person getting up from a wooden bench seat as he walked past until he heard the woman's voice, even though it was little more than a surprised whisper.

'Tom...?'

'Claire... Good heavens—' He stopped himself from saying that she was the last person he would have expected to see here but it wasn't entirely true, was it? He knew she lived close to this end of the esplanade. And saying that might make her think she was the last person he *wanted* to see here and Tom realised in that split second that that was a long way from being true as well. She was probably the only person he would have chosen to see just now. Because she would know exactly how hard this was but she wasn't so involved that it would be hard to think clearly. She could be, in fact, the kind of rock Tom very much needed in this moment.

She didn't ask him what *he* was doing here. The graze of eye contact made him think that perhaps she already knew.

'I came out for a bit of a walk on the beach,' Claire said. 'But I didn't realise how dark it was getting and I decided it probably wasn't a sensible thing to be doing on my own when there's no moonlight. I might end up in trouble if I tripped over a bit of driftwood and broke my ankle.' He could hear the smile in her voice. 'Would you like some company? You don't have to talk or anything, if you don't feel like it.'

Talking was the last thing Tom wanted to do. It took a good ten minutes of walking in a companionable silence, with only the wash of the waves and the crunch of pebbles under their feet to break it before he changed his mind.

'Olivia Jamieson was one of the first patients I ever saw at Seaview,' he told Claire quietly. 'I'd come back here to do my advanced GP training and her mum, Yvonne, brought her in for some of the usual childhood vaccinations.' He cleared his throat. 'She's got oesophageal cancer,' he said.

'Oh, no...' Claire's words were a groan. 'The worst she was expecting, according to Mabel, was that she had an ulcer from her reflux.'

'I had my suspicions that it was more than that,' Tom said quietly. 'It's rare, but neurological symptoms like the weakness and falls she presented with can be associated with an altered immune system response to a tumour. The more normal symptoms that would have raised a red flag, like a feeling that something was stuck in her throat, were masked by the issues caused by the reflux. She's booked in to start an aggressive surgical and chemotherapy regime next week in the hope of getting control.' He let his breath out in a heavy sigh. 'I'm sure I don't need to tell you what the five-year survival statistics are like.' His voice was tight. 'Yvonne asked me to go and tell Mabel and it was one of the hardest things I've ever done.'

'I'm so sorry, Tom,' Claire said.

'It broke my heart,' Tom said, his voice cracking. 'She said, "It should be me, not Livvy. I've lived my life but she's barely started. It's really not very fair, is it?".'

'No…it really isn't.' He could hear tears in Claire's voice.

They both stopped walking. He wasn't sure who initiated the hug, it just seemed to happen. They stood there in the dark, the foam of waves just catching the muted light from the streetlamps on the esplanade, simply holding each other tightly, offering and accepting comfort. An acknowledgment that they were both very personally aware of just how hard life could be sometimes.

The last of the soft strip of light on the horizon had faded by the time Claire stepped back from what was, without doubt, *the* most sincere hug she could remember getting since…well, since those unbearably dark days in the aftermath of losing Sophia.

The shared connection of that kind of pain had possibly been the beginning of the end for her marriage but with Tom it felt like the complete opposite—as if it gave them a link that was as strong as a padlock that had just been snapped shut. They both knew, too well, what it was like to have a family broken by loss and the strength that was needed to hang on long enough to rediscover the joy that was still there in being alive yourself.

One of the skills Claire had learned along the way was to deliberately look for that joy and it had become an automatic response to the touch of grief. She didn't have to look far to find it either. She just needed to tilt her head up.

'Oh, wow...' The words were an awed whisper.

Tom tilted his head back as well. 'Gorgeous, isn't it?'

'I used to think I could see the stars quite well sometimes in London, but I had *no* idea...'

'Did you know that Kaikōura has recently been officially designated as an international Dark Sky sanctuary?'

'I read something about that online. Didn't it start with some rare birds?'

Tom nodded. 'It's a type of shearwater found around Australia and New Zealand. They're the only sea bird in the world to come ashore to breed up in the mountains and this is the only place they do it. They get attracted to artificial light at night and there were too many crashing and killing themselves so a few passionate people decided to do something about controlling it. A big bonus for us is that the stars are even easier to see.'

'I wish I knew more about them,' Claire confessed. 'I can recognise the Southern Cross but everything else still looks upside down for me. That smudgy bit is the Milky Way, yes?'

Tom was just as distracted as she was, now. 'You can see it even better if you get away from the streetlights.' He caught her gaze. 'Are you up for a bit of a walk? I could show you something rather special.'

'Oh, yes, please…' The glow of something warm and happy inside Claire had finally melted that knot that had been hanging around ever since she'd noticed that Tom had been struggling with his day.

'We'll have to go up on the road, it gets a bit stony on the beach further along.' He was smiling at her. 'I wouldn't want you to fall over and break your ankle.'

There was no traffic to make it dangerous to walk along the side of the road in the dark and it became even darker as they left the last of the houses behind.

'We're heading for the oldest surviving building in Kaikōura,' Tom told her. 'It's built on a foundation of whale bones and just across the road, right on the foreshore—in the waves sometimes—is an ancient chimney which is the only part left of an old customhouse.'

He didn't take Claire onto the rocky shoreline in the dark. They leaned against the fence on the other side of the road, with Tom taking particular care to choose the exact spot to stand.

'Can you see the Milky Way now?'

'Yes…' Claire ignored the chill of the night settling around them as they stopped moving. She gazed up at the brilliance of what looked like an infinite number of stars and it was easy to find the distinctive area where the light of so many stars seemed to merge to make bright patches that emphasised the dark, smudgy band across the centre.

'Follow it down.' Tom's voice was a murmur, close to her ear. 'Until you get to the chimney.'

Claire's inward breath was a gasp of astonishment a moment later. 'It looks exactly like smoke,' she whispered. 'Coming out of the chimney.'

'Cool, isn't it?' She could hear the smile in Tom's voice. 'I remember the first time I brought Hanna out to see this. She sounded just as amazed as you do.'

They both got their phones out to take photographs of the extraordinary illusion. Then they stood for another minute, just soaking it in. Claire finally managed to drag her eyes away to look up at Tom.

'Thank you,' she said softly. 'I might never have seen this if you hadn't shown me and it's something I'll remember for ever.'

Tom just smiled. 'Thank *you*,' he said. 'Bringing you here to see this has been the best thing to happen on a really bad day.' His sigh was visible in the cold night air. 'It's the downside of spending your life as a small-town GP. You get too emotionally involved with your patients.'

'I knew it was going to be bad news when I saw you earlier today,' Claire said. 'I think that was why I ended up on the beach this evening. I was thinking about Mabel...' She paused for a heartbeat. 'I've only been here for a few weeks,' she added, 'and I already feel involved with this family myself. I can't imagine how hard it is for you.'

'I'm not very good at hiding it, am I?'

'No.' Claire smiled at him. 'You're a doctor who really cares. You're a lovely man, Tom. And a totally genuine person.'

'It's kind of my own fault that it hits me this hard.'

'What makes you think that?'

'It was my way of coping. After Jill died, I buried my own feelings by focusing on other people. Mainly Hanna, of course. But patients as well. I dealt with their problems and ignored my own. Not exactly a good way to deal with grief, is it?'

'You do whatever works,' Claire said quietly. 'Other people think they understand, but they can't, can they? Unless it's happened to them.'

'No...'

It was a negative word but somehow, it felt like an affirmation of the connection *they* had and it brought them even closer.

'It's really not a bad thing that you can't hide everything you feel for other people,' Claire said. 'It's why people love you.'

'It will be a bad thing when Hanna comes home next week for a break. If she sees us together, she's going to know straight away that I've been lying to her about you. She might be really upset about that.'

'You haven't been lying, exactly,' Claire said carefully. 'It's not as though we weren't out together when we took those photos you've been sending her. Or that we're not friends...' She hoped that was true, anyway.

'But she thinks we're more than friends. And I don't think I can pretend that it's any more than that.' Tom pushed his fingers through his hair. 'I wouldn't even know how to *begin* pretending. I haven't even *kissed* a woman since Jill died.'

His words fell into a somewhat stunned silence from Claire which she broke without thinking.

'Maybe that's a good place to start, then.' The words were out of her mouth before she could filter them. 'You never know what might happen if you push through a barrier like that. You might even meet someone you end up wanting to share your life with.'

The shocked look on Tom's face made her shake her head. 'Not me,' she said hastily. 'In the future. Hanna doesn't want you to be lonely for the rest of your life and…maybe she's right. You deserve to find whatever happiness you can in life, Tom—and…if you're hanging back because you think you've forgotten how to kiss someone then…' her heart skipped a beat '…here's your chance. There's no one to see and…it's perfectly safe.' She smiled up at him. 'I know it's purely for…um…experimental reasons. Or maybe therapeutic?'

Tom's expression had been changing as she spoke. His gaze dropped from her eyes to her lips and Claire knew he was thinking about kissing her.

Suddenly, it was exactly what she *wanted* him to do. And it had nothing to do with helping him break any self-inflicted barriers. The knot of empathy might have melted from around her heart but there was a new knot deep inside her now. Much lower down. Hotter.

Dear Lord...she fancied Tom Atkinson, didn't she?

She hadn't felt a physical attraction like this since...since for ever. It felt like it had been bottled up for her entire life and she had unwittingly just pulled the cork from the bottle.

Claire stood on tiptoes. She put her fingertips on Tom's cheek and she touched his lips with her own. Just briefly. Lightly.

'There you go,' she said very softly. 'See how easy it is?'

Tom was still staring at her lips. Then he raised his gaze to look into her eyes and she knew that it had happened for him as well. He was also feeling a potentially long-forgotten awareness of something very physical. He lifted *his* hand, but he didn't touch her cheek. He slid his hand under her hair until it was circling the back of her neck. Supporting her head as he leaned closer to put his lips on hers again.

And this time it wasn't brief. It might have started out just as light—a soft exploration of the pressure and warmth—but then it became something very different as Claire felt her lips part under Tom's and the touch of his tongue against hers.

Oh...*my*...

The barrier had well and truly been broken, hadn't it?

This was a kiss that was going to be just as memorable as seeing the Milky Way rising from a ruined chimney.

CHAPTER FIVE

FOR THE FIRST time ever, Tom Atkinson was feeling decidedly reluctant to get out of his car and start his working day at the Seaview Hospital and Medical Centre.

How on earth was he going to face Claire after last night?

After that...*kiss*.

Oh, they'd brushed it off at the time. They'd laughed about how unexpectedly successful the experiment had been and then, by tacit consent, they'd very carefully not mentioned it again for the whole of the walk back to where Tom had left his car on the esplanade, which seemed to take an inordinately long time.

And then he'd lain awake for most of the night, dealing with the emotional aftermath of embarrassment that he'd let it happen at all and guilt that he'd...well...that he'd enjoyed it so much. He was also doing his best to ignore the physical reaction that his body was trying to force him to acknowledge.

It had seemed like such a harmless idea. A practice kiss. Dipping a toe into the sea of water that actual dating might represent—because, at some level, Tom knew there was an element of truth in the idea that he was missing out on something in his life. If only he'd left it at that light, sweet brushing of lips that Claire had initiated.

But he hadn't, had he? Oh, no... Something had washed over him and rinsed away the usual impeccable self-control that Tom had put considerable effort into perfecting when it came to any interactions with women in his personal life. He'd let himself go and he'd initiated the *real* kiss. The one that had swept them both into very dangerous waters.

Good grief... How far would those currents have taken them if they hadn't both abruptly broken it off at exactly the same moment?

How on earth had it even happened? Maybe it was because he'd been totally alone with Claire, under a magically starry night sky. Or perhaps it was because they'd been pretending to go on all those dates so it almost felt...natural?

Or had it simply been because he liked Claire and he felt completely safe in her company?

No... Tom knew the reason. It had been the feeling of that touch of Claire's lips. The feeling of them moving beneath his. Alive. Responsive. The *taste* of her mouth. After so many years of being stifled—totally ignored, even—his libido had suddenly woken up and come roaring out of hibernation. Liking, laced with an undeniable appreciation of this woman's attractiveness, had suddenly morphed into something far less acceptable—like a cringemaking level of lust. The kind of hormonal overload that a teenage boy might experience.

He could only hope that Claire could excuse his lack of control. That they could, hopefully, keep it in a vaguely surprised and amused category of their friendship and sweep it firmly under the carpet. If it had been designed to counteract his inability to act like he and Claire were actually dating if they were in the same space when Hanna was visiting it had been an unmitigated failure.

If Hanna saw him being this awkward at even the thought of being in Claire's company she would, understandably, laugh out loud at the idea they'd been on any kind of date. Tom was going to have to give up the idea of using this fake dating as a protective mechanism and just confess to the deception.

He was also going to have to give up the safe cocoon of being alone inside his car. There would be patients who were already in the waiting room, ready for their appointments with him. Taking a deep breath, during which he sent up a silent plea to the universe that Claire was already busy in the treatment room or had gone on any morning house calls, he marched inside, grabbed the first set of notes Kaia held out to him and read the name on the front.

'Daphne Morris?'

'I'm here.' A middle-aged woman stood up from her chair in the waiting room.

'Come on through, Daphne,' Tom invited. The corridor looked clear, thank goodness. He could delay the moment he would have to make that first eye contact with Claire Campbell for just a little longer.

He felt even safer when he had closed the door of the consulting room behind him. 'Have a seat,' he told Daphne. 'What's brought you in today?'

'I'm feeling a bit off, Doctor. Not all the time, but quite often.'

'In what way?' Tom had opened Daphne's notes. She was a relatively new patient and he noted that she was sixty-three years old and on medication for her blood pressure and for high cholesterol.

'I get a bit dizzy and sweaty and I can feel my heart going really fast.'

Tom put his fingers on Daphne's wrist. 'It's a normal rate at the moment,' he told her. 'But let's check your blood pressure as well.' He took the cuff off the hook on the wall to wrap it around

Daphne's arm and pushed the button for the automatic measurement to start. 'How often are these episodes happening?'

'At least once every day. Sometimes more.'

'Do they happen at a particular time, like when you wake up or you're exercising or after a meal?'

'I don't think so.'

'Is there anything that makes it better?'

'I usually sit down and have a glass of water or something and it just goes away slowly.'

'Your blood pressure's fine.' Tom had been watching the figures settle. 'I'd like to listen to your chest and check your heart and lung sounds if that's okay?'

'Of course.'

Tom fitted his stethoscope to his ears. 'I might get our nurse to take an ECG as well.' He could do it himself, of course, but given the exposure needed to attach electrodes to his patient's chest, it would be preferable for it to be done, or at least chaperoned, by a female staff member. And Tom couldn't deny that there was relief to be found in the idea of a professional interaction to break the ice that seemed to have suddenly formed in his relationship with Claire. If nothing else, he'd be able to gauge how justified his worry was about the aftermath of that kiss. Maybe he was overthinking things and there was actually nothing to worry about at all?

'Take a deep breath for me, Daphne. And another one…'

There was something else he wanted to try before doing the ECG, he decided, after finding nothing of concern in what he was hearing. Or seeing. Daphne's respiration rate and skin colour were quite normal and there was no evidence of any other abnormalities like a new tremor in her hands or swelling in her ankles.

'Could you stand up for me, please, Daphne?'

His patient blinked. She looked down at the cuff still wrapped around her arm. 'Do I need to take this off?'

'No. I want to take your blood pressure and your heart rate when you've been standing up for a few minutes.'

Her blood pressure hadn't changed much after she'd been standing and answering more of his questions for several minutes but her heart rate certainly had. It had gone up from eighty to nearly a hundred and twenty beats per minute and Daphne was starting to look pale.

'I can feel it now,' she said. 'My heart's really pounding.'

'Come with me.' Tom led the way to the treatment room.

Claire had a drawer open and was taking out blood collection tubes with differently coloured tops to put into a kidney dish. There was a laboratory request form on the bench beside the dish. She looked up as Tom tapped on the door.

'You busy?'

'Just getting ready for some routine blood tests. Do you need me?'

The eye contact was brief enough to suggest that Claire was feeling just as awkward as he was. Dammit...he hadn't been overthinking things, had he?

'This is Daphne Morris,' he said, his tone a little crisper than he'd intended it to be. 'I'd like an ECG on her, please.'

'Of course.' Claire's smile was warm but it was directed at Daphne, not him. Her glance at Tom was a question. She had clearly noticed that Daphne wasn't looking so well.

'Tachycardia on standing,' he told her. 'With some vasovagal symptoms and palpitations.'

'Do come in, Daphne. This won't take long and you might feel better lying down for a few minutes.'

Claire took Daphne back to Tom's office but gave her the ECG printout to take inside by herself.

Which was fine. She did, after all, have at least one patient waiting to have their blood tests taken.

No. It wasn't really fine, was it? It would have been more professional to hand the printout of quite an impressive sinus tachycardia to Tom herself and make sure there wasn't any other assistance he required from her for this patient even if her rapid heart rate and other symptoms had subsided with rest.

But it felt so...awkward.

Claire had come to work this morning knowing that a small bomb had gone off in their personal relationship but determined not to let it affect the way they could work together. If it did, it would make what had happened last night even more of a disaster.

What on earth had made her imagine that it was an acceptable suggestion that he kissed her?

What *had* she been thinking?

Witnessing a peck on the cheek would have probably been quite enough to persuade Hanna that her father was involved in a meaningful friendship. She hadn't needed to kiss him on the lips at all, even though it had only been intended to be light enough to be insignificant.

What had happened after that, exactly?

It was a bit of a blur, to be honest. She remembered the tingling sensation that had come from that light touch and she remembered the way she couldn't look away from his eyes but she couldn't remember who had actually initiated that astonishingly passionate kiss.

Oh, dear...even the thought of it made her skin tingle. Not just on her lips but all the way down to her toes. How horrified would Tom be if he knew the effect that his kiss had had on her? Everyone knew she'd only just arrived in town. How appalled would some of them be to think that she was throwing herself at her boss? If they found out how much older than Tom she was, it would only make the gossip more juicy, wouldn't it? How had something that had been intended to make the pretence of fake dating easier gone so very wrong?

And how on earth were they going to be able to get things back to the way they *had* been? Claire didn't want to lose what she'd found with Tom. The company of someone she could have fun with. The connection with someone who really understood what she'd been through in life because he'd been there himself. Someone she enjoyed being with so much that it would leave a huge hole in her life if it vanished.

Tom's approach to sorting it became apparent later that morning, when they found themselves getting a cup of coffee in the staffroom at the same time.

'I'm going to get Daphne to come in on a regular basis for a while,' he said to Claire. 'I'd like you to do a sitting and standing blood pressure and repeat ECG. I suspect she has POTS but we'll need to monitor it for a while before I can make a definitive diagnosis.'

Claire nodded, spooning instant coffee into the mug. 'Postural Orthostatic Tachycardia Syndrome,' she said. 'Interesting...'

The condition, where the body couldn't coordinate the balancing act of blood vessel constriction and heart rate response to postural changes, was interesting. Enough to make Claire realise that Tom probably had the right idea. Focusing on their professional connection was the way to go to get things back to normal. 'Do you know what might have triggered it?'

'She hasn't had any trauma or surgery recently but she did have trouble shaking off a viral illness a while back.'

'There's no real treatment for it, is there, apart from lifestyle changes like using compression clothing and avoiding sitting or standing for too long?'

'Increasing salt intake is useful. Apparently, people who have POTS need up to three times as much sodium as the recommended limit to keep a sufficient circulating volume. Daphne was a bit horrified by that—she was more than happy to try increasing how much water she's drinking but she's been on a health kick and trying to reduce the salt and sugar in her diet.'

Keeping things professional seemed to be working, Claire decided, but then she risked a glance at Tom over the rim of her mug as she took a sip of her coffee. Just one heartbeat's worth of eye contact was enough to let her know that it wasn't actually working on anything other than a very superficial level. She didn't even need to drop her eyes to his lips to be thinking about that kiss.

Worse, to know that Tom was also thinking about it.

'I'd better get back to work.' Claire's tone was overly bright. 'I need to make some calls before the rest of my appointments for today.' She moved so quickly she was in danger of slopping her hot drink. 'I'm hoping to drop in on Mabel Jamieson on my way home and check on how she's coping after the news about Olivia.'

'Good idea.' But Tom's voice sounded as though some of his coffee might have gone down the wrong way.

Oh, help…why had she said something that was going to remind them both of the intense conversation about Mabel's granddaughter last night, which was how they'd ended up snogging like a pair of teenagers under the Milky Way?

It felt like she was scuttling out of the staff room.

If anything, the awkwardness had just got more pronounced.

Something needed to be done to break the tension that seemed to be growing rather than fading as

Tom and Claire navigated their way through the afternoon surgery hours at the same time and he found himself doing his best to avoid being in the same space at the same time, or at least avoiding eye contact if it was unavoidable. He could never have engineered the circumstances that ended up making the awkwardness suddenly becoming totally irrelevant, however.

The police car, with its lights flashing, skidding to a halt out the front door of Seaview's medical centre was dramatic enough to have the few people still in the waiting room on their feet, staring out of the windows. Tom was standing by the reception desk and Claire was coming into the room from the corridor as one of the local senior sergeants, Ngaire, rushed inside.

'We need you, Tom,' she said. Then she lowered her voice. 'Someone's been shot.'

Tom's nod was swift. So was his glance in Claire's direction. 'Can you grab the emergency kit from the treatment room, please, Claire? You'd better come too.' He turned back to Ngaire. 'Where are they?'

'Well…that's the thing. They're well up in the high country. It's an accident in a group of guys that went out deer hunting.'

Claire's steps faltered. She looked confused. So was Tom.

'What's happened to the usual emergency response via helicopter?'

'There are no rescue helicopter aircraft or crews available any time soon,' Ngaire informed them. 'We don't even have a local ambulance crew available—they're on a transfer with your man with chest pain.'

Tom nodded. He'd arranged that transfer himself.

'A Search and Rescue team, including a police officer, have already been dispatched by road,' Ngaire said, 'but it's going to take them at least an hour to reach the scene using quad bikes via the track and we've got one of the local scenic tour helicopter pilots on standby to take you there as first response. Apparently, there's a hut and an area big enough to land about a ten-minute walk away from where the victim is. There's only room for two medics and your gear but hopefully one of the rescue choppers should be available before too long for evacuation of someone on a stretcher.'

'Do you know how badly the person's injured?'

'Doesn't sound good. It's an older man who's been shot and it's a chest wound. He's having some trouble breathing but he's still conscious.'

The decision was a no-brainer. 'How soon can the pilot get to the hospital helipad?'

'Less than five minutes.'

'Right...' Tom was thinking fast. This was by no means the first time he'd been involved in a rural emergency rescue situation. He knew his colleagues would cope with any patients he couldn't see for the afternoon and he didn't want to take another doctor away from the medical centre or hospital but another qualified pair of hands might be essential. 'Change of plans, Claire,' he said. 'We'll need some extra medical supplies and some overalls and boots. For you as well. I need you to come with me. Let's see how quickly we can get sorted and out to the helipad, yes?'

If Claire Campbell was fazed by the dramatic twist in her professional duties that afternoon, she wasn't showing it. If anything, Tom had the impression that she was not only embracing the challenge but revelling in it. She moved decisively and efficiently to gather everything they had available to stabilise and monitor a critically injured patient, like a life-pack and IV gear and even a cool bag with its isothermal lining designed to keep blood products like packed red cells and fresh, frozen plasma stable for hours. She pulled on the slightly scratchy overalls on top of her scrubs with no complaints and if the sturdy boots weren't a great fit she didn't mention that either.

She did look slightly perturbed when their pilot, Jonno, did some very tight turns to show them the accident scene before going back to land on a small patch of flat ground beside a rustic mountain hut. With her eyes closed, Tom suspected that Claire probably hadn't seen the very relieved-looking hunters waving up at them.

Jonno helped them unload their gear. 'You've got the GSP coordinates loaded into your phone, yes?'

'Yep. And we've got satellite radios. If we lose the track we'll stay put and get in touch with the Search and Rescue team. They won't be too far away by now.'

'I'll keep myself available,' Jonno told them. 'But I'm guessing you'll be picked up to travel with your patient.'

Tom put the straps of a backpack over his shoulders and picked up the heavy life-pack. Claire had the container of blood products. They both reached for the oxygen cylinder at the same time.

'You've got enough to carry,' Tom said. 'I can take that.'

'I'm fine,' Claire insisted. 'I've done a lot of hiking in my time, Tom. It's not far.' She picked up the cylinder. 'And the sooner we get there, the better, yes? You lead the way. I'll be right behind you.'

They saw the group of five men huddled amongst the first line of trees on the edge of a tussock covered slope. The man on the ground was well covered with extra jackets as blankets and more clothing folded up to provide a pillow. One of them—a younger man—was sitting a little further back, his head in his hands.

'Tom!' One of the men recognised him as they got closer. 'Thank goodness *you're* here.'

'Hey, Harvey.' Tom knew him as one of their local plumbers.

'It's Bruce who's hurt,' Harvey told him. 'He's a mate of mine who came down from Wellington for a few days hunting, with his son, Mason.'

'Fill me in,' Tom said as he approached the patient. 'What happened exactly?'

'He's been shot. From a range of maybe twenty to thirty metres.' The man cleared his throat. 'One shot. Left side of his chest. No exit wound that we could see.'

The young man sitting to one side looked up, his face tear-streaked. 'It was an accident,' he said, his voice raw. 'I could see a deer in my scope. I could see its antlers…'

''Course it was, son.' The man paused to grip the younger man's shoulder. 'We all know that. We just don't know why your dad decided to leave his own patch.'

'He's going to be okay, isn't he?'

'He's got the best doctor around these parts. If anyone can help, he can... Get a bit closer, lad. Your dad'll want to see that you're here.'

From the corner of his eye, Tom could see Mason edging closer to his father as he knelt down beside the man on the ground, his fingers on the man's wrist.

'How's it going, Bruce? I'm Tom, one of the local doctors, and I've got my colleague Claire with me. We're going to get you sorted and into hospital.'

He could see, and hear, how short of breath Bruce was.

'Hurts...' he said succinctly. 'Hard...to... breathe...'

'We'll give you something for that pain asap,' Tom promised. He could see Claire attaching an oxygen mask to the cylinder and he nodded at her choice of a non-rebreather mask. Bruce had a patent airway because he was talking but they needed to try and improve his breathing before they moved on with their primary survey of how badly injured he was.

'Let's get some leads on, too,' he said calmly. 'And a set of vital signs, please, Claire.' He already knew that Bruce's blood pressure was very low because he hadn't been able to feel a radial pulse in his wrist.

'I'm going to put a mask on your face,' Claire

told Bruce. 'The oxygen should help your breathing, okay?'

Bruce nodded and Claire slipped the elastic band around his head and turned on the oxygen cylinder. She clipped a saturation monitor clip on his finger. Tom had opened the long zip on the backpack and folded it out flat to reveal all the clear plastic pouches containing supplies inside. He took out a stethoscope. Claire was folding back the layers of coats keeping Bruce warm to attach ECG electrodes below his collarbones and on the left side of his abdomen—a basic three-lead view to monitor heart rhythm and rate. Tom could see the entry wound of the bullet on the left side of Bruce's chest. Had it penetrated deeply enough to have injured his heart as well as having caused potential internal bleeding and lung damage that was affecting his ability to breathe? He would need to look for an exit wound very soon.

The screen of the life-pack was already settling as Tom placed the disc of his stethoscope on Bruce's chest and he could see that the heart's rhythm was normal but the rate was far too high at a hundred and forty beats per minute. The rate of respiration was also too high and...

'Decreased breath sounds, left side,' Tom told Claire quietly.

'SpO2 is ninety-two,' she responded. 'Up from eighty-six since the oxygen first went on.'

The level of oxygen in Bruce's blood was still too low. Already, in the space of only seconds, things were adding up and they both knew that Bruce was in trouble. The puncture wounds from the shotgun pellets were causing air, or blood—probably both—to accumulate in his chest and affect the function of his heart and lungs, which meant that not enough oxygen was reaching his vital organs. The clock was ticking and they were not in the best place to try and deal with a major resuscitation.

Bruce needed pain relief, fluids to try and increase his blood volume, drugs to try and slow any internal bleeding, to help his veins constrict to make the most of what blood was circulating and to help his heart pump more effectively.

Tom draped the stethoscope around his neck as he turned to open more pouches in the backpack.

'Have we got a blood pressure?'

'Seventy-six over forty,' Claire said. 'Also dropping.'

Tom eyed the IV cannula he'd just picked up. The only way to deliver everything was intravenously but a low blood pressure meant that access was going to be a challenge and he couldn't afford the time to try and chase a peripheral vein that might have already collapsed. He dropped the cannula and reached for a sterile package containing the device he needed to get access to the centre of a bone that could provide fast and reliable access for the infusion of both fluids and medications.

Claire was watching him. 'Insertion site?' she queried.

'Proximal tibia.'

Claire picked up a pair of shears. 'I'm going to have to cut your clothes,' she told Bruce. 'Tom's going to put a needle into your leg, just below your knee. We'll be able to give you something for that pain then. Hang in there, Bruce. You're doing well...'

Tom could feel the encouragement and warmth in her voice. If he was in as much pain as Bruce and probably terrified, he would love to hear a voice like that. It would make him feel cared for. Hopeful. Safe, even...?

Bruce made a grunting noise that sounded as if he was thinking the same thing Tom was. He had his eyes closed but he was nodding his head. 'All good,' he whispered.

'Mason's right here, too,' Claire added. 'He's the one who's holding your hand right now.'

'All...good...' Bruce repeated. 'Not...your fault...son... Mine... I forgot...where I was...'

Mason had tears streaming down his face.

'I'll need a giving set and a litre of saline,' Tom told Claire. 'And draw up a flush, too, please.'

'Onto it.'

With swift movements Tom inserted and then twisted the intraosseous needle into the tibia just below Bruce's knee and secured it. He flushed the line, attached the tubing of the giving set and asked one of the men standing around them to hold up the bag of fluid.

'Not allergic to any medications, are you, Bruce?' he asked. 'Like morphine?'

'Don't…think…so…' It sounded like it was getting harder for their patient to speak.

Tom drew up and administered pain relief. An alarm on the life-pack sounded as he was drawing up other drugs.

'Oxygen saturation is below ninety again,' Claire said. 'Heart rate's one forty and we're getting more than a few ectopics.' She gripped Bruce's shoulder. 'Can you hear me, Bruce? Can you open your eyes?'

There was no response this time.

Tom could hear other sounds from behind them. The Search and Rescue team had clearly arrived on scene now. There would be extra hands, trained in first aid to assist if needed and support Mason, who might need to be moved further away from his father very soon. The group would have carried a stretcher to the scene that could be used to carry Bruce out and get him to an emergency department and operating theatre. Hopefully fast, if a rescue helicopter became available.

They would have to stabilise him first, however, and Tom's heart sank as he discovered that breath sounds had vanished from one side of the hunter's chest and were reduced on the other side. Bruce was now unconscious and gasping for air with shallow, overly rapid respiratory efforts. His heart was throwing off unusual beats that suggested his rhythm could change, at any moment, into one that was potentially fatal, like a ventricular fibrillation.

Tom glanced up, the stethoscope still on Bruce's chest, to find Claire's steady gaze on him. She was poised to do whatever he was about to ask because she knew as well as he did that they were going to have to try something a lot more dramatic.

Bruce was in imminent danger of going into a respiratory or cardiac arrest.

And the fight for his life had just become a whole lot harder.

CHAPTER SIX

CLAIRE HAD SPENT the early years of her nursing career working in a big London hospital's emergency department.

She had seen medical experts fighting to save lives against the odds and she knew she was watching someone who knew exactly what he was doing, in an environment far more challenging than a well-equipped and staffed hospital department, as Tom worked on their patient.

Not that she was simply watching. She was as involved with this case as Tom was. His assistant. His partner.

She removed the makeshift pillows from beneath Bruce's head and positioned his arm as if to put the palm of his hand behind his head. She prepped the skin on his chest, first one side and then the other, to allow Tom to perform finger thoracostomies, where he made an incision with a scalpel and then used his finger and a pair of forceps to do a blunt dissection between ribs to reach the pleural space around the lung. A rush of air and blood escaped the channel he had created as he removed his finger. A lot of blood.

'Claire, can you find a unit of packed red blood cells and get it running, please? I'm going to decompress the other side of the chest.'

The bag of Group O blood product was smaller than the bag of saline but would be far more effective in carrying oxygen. Claire attached it to the connection on the intraosseous IV access and gave the bag to one of the men in orange overalls, who stepped forward to assist without being asked. Behind the member of the Search and Rescue team, she could see a police officer talking to the other hunters in the group. Bruce's son, Mason, was sitting to one side again, his face white as he watched what was happening around his father. Claire's heart went out to the young man, who was probably only in his late teens. He was not only afraid of losing his dad, he knew he was responsible for the accident.

It was only moments later that things started happening so fast they became almost a blur, but all Claire needed to do was to listen for Tom's voice and to do exactly what he wanted her to do.

To use an Ambu-bag to deliver breaths for Bruce, who was no longer breathing for himself, and check for a pulse that was no longer there. Even though they could see the electrical impulses on the screen of the life-pack, the heart was no longer able to pump blood.

To do chest compressions until someone else took over because she was getting tired, even if she didn't feel like she was and didn't want to stop.

To draw up and check the drugs that Tom was administering.

To do another round of chest compressions.

To hang more blood and tell the person holding it to squeeze as hard as they could to get it in faster.

To sit…much later, as daylight was beginning to fade, with her arms around Mason as he sobbed against her shoulder, while the Search and Rescue team secured Bruce's body to the stretcher so that they could carry him down the track to where they'd left their quad bikes. She only heard snatches of the orders being given and radio calls being made. It was Tom who came and crouched beside Claire and Mason.

'Hey, Mason.' His tone was so gentle that Claire felt tears spring to the back of her own eyes. 'I'm so very sorry about this. We did everything we could for your dad.'

Mason nodded without saying anything.

'We've got a helicopter coming back to collect me and Claire and our medical gear but there's enough room for you, if you'd rather come back with us.'

'But…' Mason's voice was strangled. 'What about Dad?'

'These guys, including your dad's friend Harvey, are going to carry him down the track and they've got some four-wheel drive vehicles to get back out to the main road. The police will take charge then and your dad will be taken to Christchurch and looked after while they do the kind of stuff that has to happen in cases like this.'

'I want to stay with Dad,' Mason whispered. His voice broke. 'I can help carry him.'

'That's a brave thing to do.' Claire could see the squeeze of Tom's hand as it rested on Mason's shoulder. 'Your dad would be proud of you. Harvey will look after you and your mum's going to fly down to Christchurch to be with you, too. She might even get there before you do.'

Mason nodded again. He rubbed at his nose and then scrambled to his feet. The strength he found, to not only meet Claire's gaze but to then look at Tom and even hold out a hand to shake his, was heartbreaking.

'Thanks,' he said. 'For everything you guys did. I… I know how hard you tried to save him.'

Tom took Mason's hand in his but didn't shake it. He used it to pull the younger man closer and wrap him in a brief, hard, hug.

Claire could feel the genuine empathy in that hug herself. She couldn't hold back her tears any longer but she swiped at them with her fingers and then blinked them away as she watched the team pick up the basket stretcher and start their sad journey. Mason was one of the six men who had taken hold of a cut-out hand grip.

There was a moment's heavy silence as the group vanished down the track. It was broken by Tom's voice.

'Are you okay?' he asked softly.

Claire could feel the squeeze on her heart that came from the fact that Tom had room to be concerned about *her*.

She nodded. 'I'm okay. How're you doing?'

'Oh…you know…'

She did. 'It's Mason I really feel for,' she said. 'How could it be anything other than a tragic accident? From what I picked up, they'd arranged to be hunting in totally separate blocks. Bruce had come into Mason's and he was wearing camouflage clothing. Amongst those trees it would be too easy to make a mistake. Some of those branches look exactly like antlers. And…'

With a sigh, Claire turned back to start the clean-up and packing of their gear. 'I know what it's like to feel responsible even when something isn't your fault. I spent years trying to get past the feeling of guilt that I wasn't there to help Sophia.' She put on some gloves to start picking up the bloodstained packaging and swabs but then glanced up at Tom. 'I'm guessing you know that feeling, too.'

'Yeah...' Tom echoed her sigh. 'Let's get this cleaned up and get back to the hut or Jonno will get there before us. I'll take you out for a drink when we get home—I suspect we both need a bit of a wind down. Losing a patient never gets easier, does it, even when you know you've done everything you could?'

'No...it never does...'

Claire found she could meet Tom's gaze. And hold it. As she would any colleague that she was more than happy to work with. As she would with someone who was a trusted friend as well as a colleague. She couldn't find a smile yet—the loss of their shared battle to save Bruce's life was still too raw, but being with someone who was feeling exactly the same way was possibly the only comfort to be found right now.

'A drink sounds good,' she added.

And it did. Because that awkwardness that had been there between them this morning felt like ancient history.

Along with that kiss.

Having a defined task that had to be done made it easier to cope with the aftermath of a failed resuscitation. Tom made sure that every scrap of rubbish was picked up from this patch of forest. Nobody who came this way in the future would have any idea of the tragedy that had happened here.

It was nearly dark by the time they reached the small clearing beside the hut. They piled their gear onto the small veranda of the simple wood and corrugated iron structure because there were gathering clouds and they didn't want expensive equipment like the life-pack getting wet if it started raining. They sat on the veranda step then, waiting to hear the chop of helicopter rotors in the distance and see the lights of the aircraft approaching.

Instead, they heard the crackle of the radio that Tom had.

'Tom...are you receiving? It's Jonno.'

'Receiving loud and clear,' Tom responded. 'How far away are you, Jonno?'

'I'm still in town, sorry,' he replied. 'We've got a bit of an issue with a warning light. Probably nothing but I won't be taking off until I know for sure. There's also a bit of weather blowing in and we're losing light fast so if I can't get it sorted very soon, it could be first thing in the morning before I can get back to collect you.'

'So we'll walk out?'

'Not on your own. Or in the dark. We could

send the Search and Rescue guys back up the hill but it might be a bit of a wait.'

Of course it would. The team of mostly volunteers would still be coping with their own duties and there would be protocol to follow with police interviews, probably a debriefing meeting and definitely some reports to file. The last thing those men needed was to be heading back into the mountain wilderness when it wasn't an emergency.

'We'll sit tight,' Tom told Jonno. 'We've got shelter and we can wait till morning if necessary. I don't want anyone taking any risks on our behalf.' He glanced sideways to see Claire nodding her head in agreement. 'It won't be a problem if we have to wait till first light.'

'Thanks, mate. I'll keep you posted.'

When the radio call ended there was a silence so deep it felt like he and Claire were the only people left on the planet. He caught Claire's gaze and could see that this was daunting for her but he could also see a spark of determination to cope with this challenge. To embrace it, even?

Yeah…she had an adventurous spirit, this woman.

Tom liked that.

'We may as well make ourselves at home,' he said. 'Can I make you a cup of tea?'

'You're kidding, right?'

Tom shrugged. 'You never quite know what you're going to find in a DOC hut but I wouldn't be surprised if there's a kettle and some tea. There might even be food if we're lucky.'

Claire followed his example and got to her feet. 'DOC?' she queried.

'Department of Conservation. It's a government department that oversees the care and preservation of everything to do with the land and our history. That includes the national parks and walking tracks and hundreds of huts like this one.' He turned the handle on the door and pushed it open.

'It's not locked,' Claire exclaimed.

'They're never locked. They might be needed in an emergency, if someone's injured or caught in bad weather.' He looked over his shoulder. 'Speaking of which, let's get our gear inside. That rain's going to be here any minute.'

It was more than rain by the time they got everything inside and shut the door. Hailstones were falling thickly enough to sound like machine gun fire on the corrugated iron roof and it was suddenly dark enough to feel like night had fallen.

'I get the feeling we're not going anywhere in a hurry,' Tom said.

'No.' But Claire was actually smiling as she looked around in the dim light of the hut that might have bare, rough-hewn wooden walls but it was tidy and clean. Bunk beds with sponge mattresses were on each side. In the middle was a very old potbelly stove standing on a base of red bricks and it had a pile of twigs on one side and small split logs in a box on the other. Beside that was a bench, with shelves above it that were cluttered with an eclectic mix of mugs, plastic and tin bowls and plates, a jug full of cutlery and even a wine bottle with a half-burnt candle stuck in its neck. There were bottles of water and boxes of matches, pots and frying pans and a kettle on top of the bench and cupboards underneath that revealed treasure when Tom opened them.

'There's baked beans on this restaurant's menu,' he announced. 'Or...wait for it...spaghetti. With *sausages*. That's gourmet, isn't it?'

He turned as the hiccup of Claire's laughter changed into something he recognised all too easily—the release from bottled-up emotion after an intense medical battle that hadn't been won. He'd seen Claire fighting back tears when he'd released Mason from the hug he'd used to try and convey his heartfelt sympathy but they were appearing again now and...maybe they both needed that kind of release.

'I know...' he said, holding out his arms. 'It's okay...'

He didn't need to say anything else. Tomorrow,

they could talk it through properly as they wrote the reports that would be needed into the investigation of the tragic accident and he knew they would both be left knowing they'd done their absolute best in a hopeless situation of major chest trauma and hypovolaemic shock so far away from an emergency department or operating theatre.

Offering a hug right now was the best thing he *could* do—for both of them—and he liked that Claire came straight into his arms. He knew he shed a tear or two himself as he held her for as long as it took for her to cry it out, but then it was time to be more practical.

'I'll see if I can get hold of Jonno,' he said, unclipping his radio. 'I'm guessing we're stuck here for tonight but I'm not going to light the fire until we know for sure.'

The hot tinned spaghetti in tomato sauce with the tiny, over-processed but surprisingly tasty sausages was quite possibly one of the most delicious meals Claire had ever had.

Tom had got a fire going in the little iron stove as soon as she'd finished crying all over him and the hut was now so warm she unzipped the overalls she was wearing. It was almost a surprise to realise she was still wearing her work scrubs underneath the overalls. It was only a few hours ago that she'd been in the Seaview Medical Centre doing something as mundane as taking someone's blood pressure and now, here she was in a completely different world, so far up in the mountains the rest of the world might as well have vanished.

Tom had taken a couple of the mattresses off the bunks and put them on the floor in front of the stove.

'It'll get cold in the middle of the night,' he'd warned Claire. 'I'll get a couple of foil blankets out of our kit, too, but it might be a good idea to stay here. I'll keep the fire stoked during the night. Hopefully, I'll have enough time to restock the hut before we get picked up in the morning.'

It was only then that it really hit Claire.

She was about to spend the night with Tom Atkinson.

Alone.

So far away from anyone else that they were in a world that was entirely their own.

Maybe it hit Tom at the same moment because his gaze slid sideways and his face was scrunched into lines of…was it embarrassment?

Oh, help…had that awkwardness about the kiss reared its head again?

'Sorry,' Tom muttered.

'What for?'

'You know…it's been a bit…weird today, hasn't it?'

Claire shifted her gaze to the kettle that was on the flat top of the stove, a wisp of steam curling from its spout. She wondered if she should offer to make another cup of tea which might distract them both so they could avoid this conversation. Instead, she found herself saying something else.

'It's me who should apologise. That kiss was my idea, after all.'

'Your intentions were good,' Tom said. 'Maybe I'm overreacting by being so embarrassed about it.'

'No "maybe" about it,' Claire said firmly. 'There's nothing to be embarrassed about. We're both adults, Tom. And it was just a *kiss*, for heaven's sake.'

There was a moment's silence and then Claire let her breath out in a huff. 'No…that's not entirely true, is it?' She could feel Tom's shock, but she waited a beat to deliver her punchline and turned to catch his gaze again. 'It wasn't just a kiss,' she added. 'It was a *great* kiss.'

That made Tom smile. 'It was, wasn't it? Not that I can imagine trying it with anyone else.'

'Why not?'

'The kiss made things awkward enough. How excruciating would it be if someone wanted more than a kiss and it turned out to be a disaster?'

'Why would it be?'

'I don't even know if I *could* do it.' Tom's voice

was as quiet as if he was talking to himself. 'It's been more than seven *years*.'

Claire was silent. Tom could obviously sense her astonishment.

'The world got tipped upside down,' he said. 'There was so much grief. So much effort needed to try and keep things together for Hanna. I could only focus on two things—trying to be a good enough parent to raise our beautiful girl by myself and doing the best I could for every patient that I cared for. There was no room for anything else for years and by then it was my life.' He shrugged. 'It was working. I wasn't going to risk trying to fix something that didn't actually feel broken.'

Claire nodded. 'I get it. My life fell apart too. I haven't kept count but it might have been more than seven years since *I've* had sex.'

It was Tom's turn to be astonished. 'But you only left your marriage after your sixtieth birthday party! That was only last year, wasn't it?'

Claire simply nodded. Tom could join those dots without her going into the details of a relationship that had become so distant that the thought of physical intimacy had lost any appeal.

He didn't say anything for some time. He stoked the stove and then made them a mug of tea and they sat there in a silence that was perfectly companionable.

More than companionable, really. They'd shared a rather intimate confession that gave them rather an unusual connection, hadn't they?

It was Tom that finally broke the silence. 'Do you think you could ever get that close to someone again?' he asked.

Claire thought about that for a long moment. 'A year or so ago I would have definitely said no, but...you know what?'

'What?'

This was a new thought for Claire. A seed that had only just sprouted—possibly thanks to this conversation, even.

And it was a thought that was...rather thrilling, to be honest.

'I'm starting to think that I can do anything I want with the rest of my life,' she said, a little shyly. 'Look at me—I'm living on the other side of the world and right now, I'm nearly on top of a mountain in the middle of nowhere. If I meet the right person, at the right time, I might just forget that I'm too old to be doing anything as silly as sex and I might just jump in and have some fun.'

'You're not too old.' Tom was smiling, as if he was picking up on the embryonic excitement that Claire was feeling. 'And you *can* do whatever the hell you want. Hey...isn't sixty the new forty?'

Claire snorted. 'Not according to my bathroom mirror when I get out of the shower every morning.'

'You're beautiful, Claire,' Tom said quietly. 'Inside and out. We should both be past an age where what we look like matters. Who cares about a few wrinkles or scars or flabby bits?'

'I *don't* care,' Claire said. 'Not really. I'm happy and healthy and that's what really matters.' But she hunched her shoulders in an extreme wince. 'It's just the thought of some stranger judging me when I take my clothes off that's really off-putting.'

'That doesn't bother me as much as what happens after that,' Tom confessed. 'The…ah…performance factor? Especially the first time. What if it's too much to handle and…*nothing* happens? It would be the first *and* last time for me.'

'You can't let that happen.' Claire was shaking her head. 'The first time *is* going to be huge and if it's too much, so what? If you're with someone that you trust—someone that understands how huge it is, you can just try again. Take it slowly. Take as long as you need.' She offered Tom a slightly apologetic smile. Who was she, after all, to be offering advice on a subject like this? 'I'm older and wiser than you,' she added. 'And…and I think you deserve to have more in your life. Maybe Hanna's right to give you a push. This is *my* push.'

Tom was staring at her. 'You kissed me,' he said finally, so softly she could barely hear the words over the crackle of the fire as he opened the door of the stove to add more wood. 'I didn't expect that it would make me feel like it did.' He closed the door and turned to face Claire. 'Like... I wanted more.'

Claire swallowed hard. She'd wanted more, too, hadn't she? She could remember every detail of that kiss. She could feel the curl of sensation deep in her belly that was the spark of desire that was about to catch fire like those logs in the little potbelly stove.

She had no idea how long they simply stared at each other. She could see something in Tom's eyes that told her he was feeling something similar but he wasn't going to say anything more, she realised. This was her choice. If she didn't say anything herself, the whole subject of sex would never be spoken about again.

She dropped her gaze so that she could think about this without being distracted by how unbelievably attractive this man was and she discovered that there was something more than just the fizz of simmering desire that she was aware of. It was that thought she'd told Tom about—that she could do anything she wanted with her life from now on. If she wasn't brave enough to do something that scared her, how on earth would she know whether she was really making the most of her life?

Judging by the way her heart had picked up enough to feel like it was hammering against her ribs, this was absolutely scary. But what was the worst that could happen here?

Something embarrassing, that's what. But they were friends. They trusted each other. They could laugh that off, surely?

Her voice sounded oddly rough when she spoke.

'If you wanted,' she said slowly, thinking out loud. 'We're in the perfect place to have a trial run. Nobody else would ever have to know.' She let her gaze touch his. 'What happens in the hut would stay in the hut, wouldn't it?'

Tom was staring at her again. She could see the muscles in his throat moving as he swallowed. Carefully.

'Of course it would,' he agreed.

The candle in the wine bottle was giving its final flickers but neither of them got up to find a new one from the supply on the shelf beside the matchboxes. The light coming through the grilles of the metal door in the stove was bright enough to give things in close range a rosy glow, but it was soft enough for Claire to be confident that most physical imperfections would be almost invisible. The shadows further back made the bunk beds and everything else in the hut irrelevant and the sound of heavy rain on the iron roof was a barrier to the outside world that made this little patch of warmth and light the only patch of the planet that mattered in this moment.

And they were the only people that mattered.

This was crazy.

But all Tom could think of in this moment was *that* kiss—and how it had made him feel as if he wanted more.

As if he wanted *everything*...

And here it was, being offered to him with no strings attached whatsoever. With the most complete privacy you could ever imagine and a promise that nobody else would need to know about it if it didn't work.

There was a flicker of something in Claire's eyes that he'd never seen before. Not fear exactly, but he had the impression that it had taken rather a lot of courage for her to make this offer.

And maybe...she needed a trial run as much as he did?

Claire Campbell had left an unhappy marriage and her old life behind and she was planning to have adventures and make the most of whatever life she had left to live. He'd heard that shy note of hope in her voice when she'd confessed that maybe she *would* be happy to find someone to get close to again. To have some fun with.

To have *sex* with.

Maybe she was as nervous as he was at the prospect, even if it was for different reasons. Claire had no reason to feel like her body would be less than desirable in any way but he could understand why she might need reassurance. Like him, she hadn't been physically intimate with anyone in a very long time.

They could help each other.

It could, in fact, be a gift that would keep giving for the rest of their lives.

He held her gaze. 'Are you sure about this?'

Her eyes looked enormous and so dark they were unreadable but her expression was very serious. 'Yes.' Then a hint of a smile lifted the corners of her mouth. 'Fortune favours the brave,' she said.

'Nothing ventured, nothing gained,' Tom responded. He could feel a smile of his own trying to emerge.

Claire was really smiling now. 'Who dares wins,' she offered.

'No guts, no glory,' Tom countered.

'Do one thing every day that scares you.'

'Good grief...we're starting to sound like social media memes.'

They were both laughing now, but the sound

faded and their faces stilled at the same time as well, until they were both simply looking at each other in the semi-darkness with no more than the glow of the firelight.

Tom reached out to brush strands of Claire's silver hair back from her face. She tipped her head to nestle her cheek into the palm of his hand and the movement was so trusting, so *welcoming*, that Tom could feel his whole body responding. He kept his hand there, cupping her face, and leaned closer to touch her lips with his own.

It was like that kiss on the beach under the millions of stars. A whisper of sensation that was all that was needed to conjure up the swirling currents of waters that didn't seem nearly as dangerous now. They knew what they were doing. They didn't have to control themselves and back off because they both wanted this. They undressed each other in the warmth still radiating from the stove. They smiled about not needing to worry about protection.

'Don't they say that you're a born-again virgin when it's been so long since you've had sex?'

'No need to worry about an accidental pregnancy either. There's a plus side to getting older, isn't there?'

There was certainly a plus side to the laughter. The fear of embarrassment was evaporating with every kiss. Every touch. Tom's body was letting him know that it remembered exactly how this worked and Claire seemed to be as lost in this almost forgotten world as he was rapidly becoming. His last coherent wish was that this would give Claire all the confidence she needed to know that she could do anything she wanted in the future.

His wish for himself was very simple.

He wanted *this*...

This moment. This feeling of being truly alive again for the first time in too many years.

And he wanted *this* woman.

Claire...

He didn't realise he'd spoken her name aloud until she responded.

'I'm here,' she whispered. 'Oh, Tom... I want you... *Now*...'

CHAPTER SEVEN

Jonno arrived in his helicopter to collect them not long after dawn the next day.

'Sorry about that,' he said. 'Turned out it was the warning light that was faulty but by the time we discovered that, the storm was on top of us.' He shook his head as he looked from Tom to Claire and back again. 'Doesn't look like you guys got much sleep.'

Claire made sure she didn't catch Tom's gaze by stooping to pick up the oxygen cylinder in one hand and the life-pack in the other. They hadn't got much sleep, but if Jonno knew the real reason why he would be horrified. Their pilot was still young enough to probably think that people her age wouldn't even be interested in sex any longer, let alone stay awake long enough to repeat—and embellish—what had been the best sex ever as far as Claire was concerned, anyway.

They landed at Seaview Hospital's helipad and found people waiting for them as they walked through the doors of the medical centre. One of them was Ruby, who was in charge of the hospital's kitchen.

'You must be starving,' she said. 'I've got bacon and eggs waiting for you in the kitchen. Unless you want a shower first?'

'A quick shower would be great,' Claire said. Did she look as dishevelled as she felt? Like a woman who'd thoroughly enjoyed an unexpectedly passionate sexual adventure?

Which was all it had been. A trial run for both of them. There was no need for it to ever happen again, so there was no need for anyone else to know anything about it...

What had happened in the hut was definitely going to stay in the hut.

But it had not only been a revelation for Claire, it had opened up a whole new level in her plan to make the most of the rest of her life. She'd never had any idea that sex could be *that* good...

'Sorry, what...?' She realised she'd completely missed what Ian, one of the other doctors in the team, had just said.

'You've got about an hour to get cleaned up and have something to eat. Lots of coffee might be a good idea, too. There's a specialist police team from Christchurch who are already on their way here to interview you both about your part in the incident.' He shook his head. 'Sounds like a real tragedy. Any hunting accident is awful, but for a son to have killed his father...how could anyone get past that?'

Claire suddenly felt guilty that she and Tom had managed to distract themselves from the tragedy so effectively for those night-time hours. Not that it mattered, but had that been partly why it had happened at all? Because they both needed an escape from the worst aspects of their work and something overwhelmingly physical was guaranteed to stop them lying awake and thinking about the awful moments of losing their fight to save a life?

Tom's response was a grunt that let Ian know he wasn't ready to discuss it yet.

'Thanks for stepping in for me,' he said. 'Any emergencies or issues with our inpatients?'

'Only Mrs B sleepwalking again. She thought someone had left the gate open and the sheep were all out on the road. She almost got as far as the road before Cathy noticed her bed was empty. It's probably time to think about transferring her to a secure dementia care facility.'

Tom nodded. 'In the meantime, we need an alarm of some kind. One of those mats that can go beside the bed and gets activated with any weight going onto it should do the trick. But the doors were all locked, weren't they?'

'She figured out how to open the fire door.'

'Let's make sure it's on the agenda for our next

staff meeting. I'll have a chat to the family later today. Was that the only excitement?'

'Thankfully, yes...but there is another patient I want to talk to you about...'

Claire left them to it. She went into the staff locker room that included a shower and stood under the rain of hot water for quite some time. She was tired, of course, and emotionally drained after the adrenaline rush of yesterday's mission. Her body felt different, too—her arm and leg muscles were a bit sore after the unfamiliar activity of carrying heavy gear over a rough track. She could feel other parts of her body, too, that had been well-used for the first time in too many years.

But...she felt better than she had in even longer than that. As if she'd ridden an emotional—and physical—rollercoaster and the buzz hadn't yet worn off. She felt exhilarated and more alert than she could believe possible after so little sleep.

After the shower, she got dressed in the clothes she'd come to work in yesterday and used a comb and a lipstick that were in her bag to try and make herself look presentable for the interview that was going to happen before she could go home to start what was rostered to be a day off for her. She checked her reflection in the mirror as she turned to leave the locker room and she saw something that made her blink. And then smile.

She looked...alive, she decided. Really alive. And happy.
Really happy.

Tom and Claire were interviewed separately. Claire had been first and had been told she could go home afterwards, which was good because she had to be as exhausted as he was.

Not that Tom was going to allow himself to think about why they were both so tired. He needed every ounce of his concentration to detail everything that had happened from the moment they'd arrived at the scene of the dreadful hunting accident. The interview was being recorded. Questions were being asked.

'The man who organised the hunting trip—Harvey Blakely, is a local plumber. You know him, yes?'

'I do.'

'We interviewed him last night. He was a close friend of the deceased and came to Christchurch to support the son, who is allegedly the person who fired the fatal shot.'

Tom gave a single nod although he hadn't been asked a question.

'Harvey told us that he could see the machine you were using to record vital signs and that he could see a heartbeat on the screen. He said he had complete faith in how you were treating the victim—that your reputation as a doctor is second to none—but he couldn't understand why you started doing CPR.'

'There was no pulse,' Tom explained. 'Which meant that there was no blood circulating so there was no oxygen to keep cells alive. He wasn't breathing. And yes, there was a rhythm to be seen on the screen for some time, but it's a rhythm called PEA. Pulseless Electrical Activity. The electrical signal for the heart to pump was still being generated but it wasn't making the heart pump.'

'Why not?'

'In this case, I suspect it was hypovolaemic shock from internal bleeding. Despite our efforts to replace fluid volume with saline and the blood products, he was still bleeding into his chest cavity. Has the autopsy been done yet?'

'It's happening today.'

'I'd appreciate a copy of that, if that's okay.'

'Of course. We'll supply the coroner with all the details you've given us of your treatment and the drugs administered etcetera. We also have your assistant, Claire Campbell's statement.' The police officer looked up at Tom from the papers in front of him on the table. 'She thinks very highly of your judgement and capabilities.'

It was the first gleam of something warm in what had been a difficult interview, going over every tiny detail of a resuscitation that had failed. Knowing that Claire respected his abilities this much gave him a glow of pride.

'I would say the same about hers,' Tom said. 'She hasn't been working here very long, but she is the best practice nurse I've ever had the privilege of working with.'

'That's the impression everyone seemed to have at the scene.' The other police officer was nodding. 'They all said you seemed to be a great team. That you knew what you were doing. And that it was obvious you did everything you could to save the victim.' Her face creased into lines of sympathy. 'I'm sorry it was unsuccessful. I'm also sorry you had to be left out there for the night. I hope it wasn't too much of an ordeal.'

Tom merely shook his head, with a smile that dismissed the experience as something prolonged and memorably unpleasant.

He had to admit, as he walked to his office a few minutes later, that it had certainly been memorable. And it had been prolonged enough to leave him feeling distinctly sleep-deprived. But it had been the polar opposite of unpleasant. The very thought of it was enough to make his entire body tingle.

There was a twinge of regret to be found in the thought that it was never going to happen again.

That what had happened had been left behind where it had happened. In the hut.

He almost bumped into Claire in the corridor as she was coming out of the treatment room.

'How did it go?' She grimaced. 'Silly question, sorry. I think I'm too tired to be thinking straight.'

'It's your day off, isn't it?'

'Yes, I'm just heading home. I'll sleep for a while and then have a long walk on the beach, I think.'

'Sounds good.'

Claire opened her mouth as if she was about to say something else, but then she bit her lip as if she felt she shouldn't. Tom knew she'd been about to invite him to join her. And that tingle in his body had suddenly ramped up into something else—a stab of sensation that was strong enough to be almost a physical pain.

It felt like he'd hit a wall that was stopping him from being able to do something that he really, really wanted to do and he also knew what that was. He wanted to touch Claire again.

To make love to her. Again.

Was it possible that what he was feeling was so strong that it was radiating into the air between them?

Because when he held Claire's gaze for a heartbeat too long, it felt like she was feeling it as well.

Tom tried, and failed, to keep his tone light. Friendly, even.

'I'd love to join you,' he said. 'But I need to have some more coffee and a shower and get on with my day.'

A cold shower might be a good idea, he thought as the corners of Claire's mouth turned up into the softest smile he'd ever seen on her face.

'Maybe next time,' she murmured, turning to walk away.

Tom watched her disappear into the waiting room. He wasn't quite sure whether that had been an actual invitation but he was sure of something. There *was* going to *be* a next time.

And that made him feel good.

Really good.

It was there every time they were breathing the same air.

Claire could feel the chemistry actually happening. The mix of components was far more powerful than it had been when she'd first been aware of how attractive Tom was, because there were memories stirred into it now. Memories of that first kiss under the stars and of making love in the glow of a small potbelly stove in a mountain hut. Memories that never failed to spark a physical reaction. Claire could feel her heart rate pick up every time she saw Tom in the days following that night in the hut. She could feel something melty happening in her gut if she was close enough to pick up the scent of his skin or if he was holding a door open for her to walk through, perhaps. It was felt more fiercely if their hands happened to brush, like they had when they'd reached for a set of patient notes on the reception desk at the same time, for example. It was astonishing that nobody else seemed to be aware of what had happened and the new level of connection there was between herself and Tom.

Apart from Tom, of course.

Claire knew he was not only aware of it, he was feeling it himself. She could see a flash of it in even the briefest eye contact. She could feel it in some indefinable difference in the way he smiled at her. They were both doing their best to ignore it, however. Were they both hoping it would simply fizzle out? Or were they waiting so as not to be the one to suggest...

What...another fake date?

Except...there would be nothing fake about what would happen if they ended up alone together again, would there? And maybe that was what was stopping them. Now that they'd included sex in the pretence, it felt different. More complicated.

Dangerous?

No… Nobody was going to end up getting hurt. A serious relationship was the last thing Tom wanted. That had, after all, been the whole point of starting the fake dating in the first place. And Claire? Well, she didn't want anyone getting in the way of all the adventures she intended having, thank you very much.

So…while there wasn't any real reason to repeat what had happened in the hut, there wasn't really any reason *not* to either. *Que será, será*, she decided. And in the meantime she intended to quietly enjoy the frissons of physical attraction that hummed in the air between herself and Tom. She was blissfully confident that nobody around them had any idea of what she might be thinking—until the following week when she finished a brief conversation with Tom at the desk as he was searching for a patient's email address and turned to find his daughter Hanna in the waiting room.

Watching them.

Her smile felt oddly wary. 'Hey…it's Hanna, isn't it? Hi! I don't think we've ever been properly introduced.' They'd never been introduced at all, had they? She'd just eavesdropped on this young woman having an altercation with her father. 'I'm Claire…'

'Oh, I know…' Hanna's smile was amused.

'I'd recognise you anywhere after all the photos Dad's been sending me.'

'I'll be out in two minutes,' Tom told his daughter as he finished scribbling down the address he'd been searching for on a scrap of paper. 'I just need to flick off a quick email.'

'I'm taking the afternoon off,' he told Claire as she followed him out of the reception area. 'Hanna wants to fish from the boat and I'm going to go diving for some crayfish.' He paused by his office door. 'She also wants you to come for dinner,' he said quietly. 'At our place.' He raised an eyebrow. 'If you're not busy?'

He held Claire's gaze long enough to let her know that Hanna had decided it was time for her to meet the woman her father was supposedly dating. This could be the end point in this pretence if Hanna guessed the truth. No wonder Tom was looking as wary as Claire had felt when she saw that Hanna was back in town.

But things were different now. The awkwardness of that kiss was long gone. In its place was this simmering attraction that made it more than pleasant to be close to this man. It shouldn't be at all difficult to convince Hanna that their dating wasn't fake.

'I'd love to come,' she said. She held *his* gaze for a moment longer, hoping to convey a reassuring message. 'Crayfish? Yum… I hope it's a very successful fishing trip.'

The crayfish were lined up on the kitchen bench as Tom prepared to cook them. He had a pot of water coming to the boil to blanch them and the grill was on in the oven to finish them off. He would heat the frying pan as well soon and melt the butter to cook the fish fillets waiting on a plate beside it.

Hanna and Claire were at the kitchen table, sipping white wine and finishing off the preparation of a salad to go with their dinner. They'd been talking about Hanna's plans for her future studies.

'I'll know before Christmas if my application to med school has been successful. If it isn't, I'll have to do something else.'

'What would you do?' Claire asked.

'Keep going with a science degree and reapply as a graduate. Or maybe I'll become a nurse, like you. You like your job, don't you?'

'Love it,' Claire said. 'Nursing is a fabulous career. Especially these days, when you can become a nurse practitioner and get to do a lot of what used to only be done by doctors. I suspect you really want to be a doctor, though, like your dad?'

'I do.' Hanna sighed. 'I hope I get in.'

'I'm quite sure you will,' Tom said. 'But it

wouldn't be the end of the world if you had to wait a bit longer, would it? I know you're the same age I was when I went into medicine, but seeing you sitting in the boat this afternoon, waiting to feel your fishing line announce a catch, you looked exactly like you did when you were about fourteen years old and we'd take the boat out at least twice a week.'

'They were good days.' Tom saw Hanna glance up, from where she was about to start slicing a sourdough loaf, to smile at Claire, who was now crumbling some feta cheese on the top of the salad. 'It became our thing, after Mum died. When we'd had a bad day, we'd go out on the boat for hours. Sometimes we didn't catch anything but it didn't matter. We always felt better when we got back and usually we had crayfish for dinner. Like tonight.'

He liked the soft way Claire smiled back at Hanna.

It stirred something very deep and his breath caught as he realised what it was. The last time he'd been in this kitchen with Hanna and a woman had been when Jill had still been alive—and well enough to be eating at the kitchen table.

It brought back such powerful memories of... family that Tom braced himself for the familiar shaft of grief that could still catch him unawares. But it didn't come. Was that because he knew he wasn't betraying the memory of Hanna's real mother by having any intention of replacing her? Claire was here as a friend, nothing more, so perhaps that was why he wasn't feeling sad. Or guilty. If anything, he was feeling grateful for being reminded of something special.

That bond between people that only family could create.

He turned to flick on the gas burner beneath the frying pan. He couldn't see Claire's smile now but he could hear its gentleness in her voice.

'Sounds like the perfect way to deal with grief. I can see why you and your dad have such a close bond. Did you get into scuba diving, too?'

'I tried it when I got older but I prefer sitting on top of the waves and breathing real air.'

'I'd be the same,' Claire said fervently. 'I went snorkelling once and I hated breathing underwater for just a single breath at a time—it felt *so* wrong. Terrifying, even.'

She got up and came close to Tom to rinse her hands under the kitchen tap. So close, his arm brushed hers as he reached for the garlic and butter he would need to add to the crayfish when they were under the grill. The touch of her skin gave him what felt like a mild electric shock and, judging by the way Claire's glance caught his so quickly, she'd felt it as well.

Maybe it was just as well Hanna was visiting.

It might be inevitable that he and Claire were going to enjoy the kind of pleasure they'd reminded themselves about in that mountain hut but it wasn't going to be tonight.

It was Claire that broke that rather intense eye contact. She eyed the shellfish as she reached for a paper towel to dry her hands.

'They're enormous,' she said. 'Were they hard to catch? Do they try and nip you with their claws?'

'It can be a challenge,' Tom said. 'They hide under rocks and all you can see are the antennae. You have to sneak up on them and get as close as you can before you try and grab them—behind the horns at the bottom of the antennae. You have to have a good hold, too, or they can scoot backwards and escape.'

Claire laughed. 'You sound like you love the chase.'

'You're not wrong there.'

He loved the sound of Claire laughing, too. It was impossible not to smile himself.

'Maybe you should have a go at proper diving,' he said. 'Pete's a great teacher. You might change your mind about breathing underwater and learn to love it, too.'

She shook her head. 'Don't think so. I'd like to go out on a boat soon, though. I'll have to chase up Carl and remind him to let me know when it's going to be a good day to go whale watching.'

Tom used tongs to take the crayfish from the boiling water and then cut them in half to put under the grill.

'Dinner's going to be ready in about five minutes,' he said. 'Could you set the table, please, Hanna?'

'That was *so* good, Dad. You've become a really good cook, you know that?'

'Oh...thanks, Hanna. Glad you liked it. I think Claire did, too.'

He'd rebuffed Claire's offer to help clean up, persuading her to go home before it got too late. The dinner had been a resounding success and he'd been delighted that Claire and Hanna had got on so well with each other, but the more time they spent together, the higher the risk that Hanna might pick up on something and realise that things weren't quite what they might seem.

Hanna was nodding happily. And then she smiled broadly. 'She likes more than just your cooking, that's for sure.'

Tom threw her a swift glance. 'What do you mean?'

Hanna laughed. 'I saw the way you two were looking at each other when she was washing her hands. I almost offered to disappear and give you some alone time but I was enjoying getting to know her. She's really nice, Dad. I like her.'

'Yeah…' Tom put another plate onto the rack for Hanna to dry. 'I do, too. She's great company.'

'Looked like more than just great company to me. I reckon I could see some pretty decent sparks flying around between you two.'

Oh, *man*…they'd been too successful in trying to convince Hanna that something was going on, hadn't they? And, as far as he'd thought, they hadn't even been trying to pretend they were dating this evening. If anything, they'd been trying to hide how close they'd accidentally become last week.

'And didn't I hear that you were both stuck overnight in that mountain hut?'

Tom almost dropped the plate he was lifting from the sink. Was Hanna reading his mind?

'Where did you hear *that*?'

'Everybody's been talking about it. Harvey the plumber was in Beachcombers the other night and when I had coffee with Kerry this morning she gave me a rundown about what he'd been saying to some of his mates when he got upset after a few beers. The helicopter pilot who was supposed to pick you up was there, too, but they weren't just talking about you and Claire getting stuck. Did you really poke huge holes in the chest of that guy who got shot?'

Tom sighed. 'He had major injuries. I did finger thoracostomies to try and decompress his chest.'

'Wow... I'm going to go and look for some videos online. That sounds like some hardcore first aid.'

'You could say that.' Tom's tone was dry and at least Hanna had been diverted from trying to find out just how close he had become to Claire.

Or had she?

'So...you and Claire...'

Tom didn't want to discuss it. Giving the impression that he had indeed been dating Claire had been surprisingly effective this evening but Hanna was his daughter. She'd see through any pretence if she asked too many questions. And then he'd have to confess the deception and she'd be really hurt, even if he explained that he'd done it because he didn't want her to be worried about him.

But she'd also be hurt on *his* behalf if she thought he was in a real relationship and it ended in the not-too-distant future, wouldn't she?

'It's early days,' he said, carefully slotting the last of the cutlery into the rack and pulling the plug from the sink. 'We're good friends, that's all. I don't even know how long Claire's going to be here. She's planning on having adventures for the rest of her life. She might not want to stay in one place.'

'She might change her mind,' Hanna said. 'Especially if you stop giving her mixed messages.'

'What's that supposed to mean?'

'You're still wearing your wedding ring, Dad.' She caught his gaze, her voice soft. 'That's like a "No Trespassing" sign for most women. A barrier to being anything more than good friends, that's for sure.' She put the dry cutlery into the drawer in front of her. 'I'm assuming Claire's been married. She's not wearing a ring.'

'No. She threw it away. Into the Thames. Her husband was cheating on her.'

Hanna looked impressed 'Go Claire.' She grinned. 'I like her even more now.' Then her tone softened. 'Don't you think it might be time to take yours off?' she suggested. 'Mum would have wanted you to be happy, you know. And I think Claire makes you happy.'

Tom pulled in a slow breath. It was true. He did feel happy when he was with Claire. This certainly wasn't the moment to confess that they'd only been pretending to be dating. And…hadn't he thought that maybe he was ready to think about the possibility of another relationship? Removing his wedding ring would be the logical first step in that direction but…

'I *can't* take it off,' he told Hanna. 'See?' He

tugged the gold band, which didn't get anywhere near his knuckle. 'It's too tight and I don't want to damage it by cutting it off.'

'But would you take it off if you didn't have to cut it?'

'I...' Tom thought of how happy he'd looked in that photo on the day they'd gone to see the baby seals. How he'd felt the yearning to have that kind of companionship in his life again. 'Yes...' he said slowly. 'I think I would.'

'It's been a shield,' Hanna said. 'Be honest. You've used it to put women off. You're still using it.'

He couldn't deny it. And he knew that Hanna could see the truth in his face by the look she gave him. 'Don't move,' she commanded. 'I'll be right back.'

She came back, holding a dental floss dispenser. She broke off a long thread and pushed one end of it under Tom's ring by putting pressure on the ring from beneath to create a gap. She wound the length tightly around his finger from the ring to his fingernail.

'You do realise you've cut off my circulation? Look—my nail's gone completely blue. I'd quite like to keep this finger.'

'Hold your horses. This is the magic bit.' Hanna picked up the loose end on the other side of the ring and began to unwind it. The thread pushed the ring further along the compressed finger with every new loop, over the knuckle and then...and then it was off. His finger was bright red and there was a deep groove where the ring had been for more than twenty years, but it was off. Hanna handed it to him and then gave him a fierce hug.

'Put it somewhere with your other treasures that remind you of Mum,' she said. 'But it's okay to move on, Dad. It's okay to fall in love again and not be lonely for the rest of your life.' She let him go and swiped at a tear that was trickling down the side of her nose. 'I really hope it lasts with you and Claire,' she said. 'For what it's worth, I think she'd make an awesome stepmum. And, more importantly, I think you're perfect for each other.'

Tom watched her walk out of the kitchen.

What on earth had just happened?

And why did it feel like Hanna might be right?

Not about him and Claire being perfect for each other, but about it being time to be honest.

Pretending to still be married by continuing to wear that ring had not been honest.

Pretending to be in a genuine relationship with Claire was not being honest either.

But Hanna was so happy about it. And she was proud of him for making an effort to move on with his life. He'd hate to see that replaced by disappointment at his being less than honest.

Maybe Claire would have a good idea of how to fix this?

CHAPTER EIGHT

'I DON'T THINK it really needs fixing.'

Claire and Tom were using the bonus of a longer than normal lunch break to have a brisk walk up to the lookout and back. They'd invited everyone else in the staffroom to join them for some fresh air and exercise before the afternoon surgery began but nobody was keen. Kaia said she would be getting all the exercise she needed when she went to her line dancing class in the evening and Ian said he was going surfing after work.

Thanks to it just being the two of them, and possibly because they were retracing their footsteps to the site of the first fake date photo that they'd taken for Hanna's benefit, Tom had told Claire about the conversation he'd had when he and Hanna had been washing the dishes after the dinner she'd been invited to a few days ago.

'And I'm starting to think she's right—it's dishonest to let her think we're really dating. It's been playing on my mind a lot. I've never been anything less than honest with her—even when it was the hardest thing in the world—like when I had to tell her that her mother wasn't going to get better.'

'I wouldn't say it's dishonest.' Claire was having to push herself to keep up with Tom's long strides and her breathing rate was increasing. 'All you've done is send her photos of places we've actually been to together.'

'It was easier when it was only text messages. Before she'd met you. She really likes you, by the way.'

'I really like *her*.'

The look she received was a question she knew Tom was unlikely to ask aloud. So she told him, anyway.

'It used to be so hard to talk to girls who are around the same age that Sophia was when she died. She'll be eighteen for ever in my heart. But now, with enough time that's gone past, there's a special kind of joy in being reminded. It's new and different but it's familiar enough to fill a hole with something that I've missed *so* much.'

The question in Tom's eyes had vanished. Instead, the softness suggested that he understood completely. That he was happy his daughter could do that for her.

'She's a credit to you, Tom,' Claire added. 'And

I'll bet she'll end up being just as brilliant a doctor as her dad is.'

'She knows about the night in the mountain hut.'

'*What?* You told her about that? That we'd...?' She couldn't bring herself to finish her sentence. What would she call it? Having sex? Having a trial run to see whether they'd forgotten how to do it? Making love...?

'*No!*' Tom sounded horrified. 'Of course I didn't. She'd heard about it from her friend Kerry—the one who works at Beachcombers. Apparently, Harvey got a bit tearful when he was having a few beers with his mates and he was telling them how traumatic it all was. And Jonno was there, too, but it was already common knowledge that he hadn't been able to get back to pick us up.'

'What did *you* say?'

'That we're just good friends. That you'd probably be moving on at some point to have a new adventure somewhere else.'

'There you go, then... You were perfectly honest.'

'She told me I wasn't being honest by still wearing my wedding ring. So I took it off. Or rather, she did. I think she wanted to see if the dental floss trick would work.'

They'd reached the top of the hill now and

Claire really needed to catch her breath so they stood there in silence for a minute or two. There was less snow on the mountains than there had been the last time they'd come up here and the cool breeze was welcome after the speed of their walking. In the sunshine, the sea was an even more glorious shade of turquoise near the shore.

Claire had noticed the day after that dinner that Tom wasn't wearing his wedding ring any longer but she hadn't said anything. It had, in fact, given her an odd sensation—as though she'd taken too deep a breath, too quickly. As if the road she was on had suddenly turned an unexpected corner. She'd wondered if the decision had had anything to do with her. She'd even wondered if she *wanted* it to have anything to do with her.

What if the age gap between herself and Tom wasn't as important as she thought it was?

What if she didn't really want to be floating from one place to another for the rest of her life, having adventures but never putting down roots or sharing her life in a meaningful way with anyone else?

What if fake dating could turn into *real* dating?

No...she didn't want that. Did she? But even if she did, Tom didn't feel the same way. He was feeling guilty that he hadn't been honest enough with his daughter—that she should know this was not a real relationship. And it never would be? That thought took her right back to her first comment about his concerns.

'I still don't think it's something that needs fixing,' she said. 'It's going to fix itself without you having to confess anything because I *will* be moving on eventually. There's too much to see out there. Have you seen that video that's gone viral? The one that was filmed from the cockpit of a plane as it dodged mountains and then followed the lake to land at Queenstown Airport? You were absolutely on point when you said it's a place I shouldn't miss.'

Tom threw her a smile. 'We were standing right here when I said that, weren't we? Feels like a long time ago.'

It had felt fake then. Claire remembered how she'd pasted that big smile on her face and tilted her head so that it was touching Tom's shoulder while he took the selfie. She remembered how nice it had felt to have his arm around her for the first time.

She'd had *no* idea how it was going to feel to be even closer to him.

And, dammit...she wanted to be that close again.

She tried to shake off the longing. She shaded her eyes with her hand and stared out to sea. 'Can't see any whales.'

'Maybe next time. We'd better start heading back, anyway.'

'We'd get fit if we did this a bit more often.' Claire pulled in a deep breath of the clear air. 'We could start climbing those mountains if we kept it up.'

'That's not a bad idea. I've been thinking I should get up there and restock the firewood we used. And take a box of canned food to go in the cupboards in case someone else needs it one day.'

'Sounds like we'll be carrying some heavy packs. We'll have to get really fit.'

It would take lots of long walks up hills to do that. Afternoons or whole days off spent on the tracks near the rivers and forests of the wilder country that was on their doorstep. The prospect was more than appealing but Tom's expression was almost a grimace.

'Yeah… That might be stretching things a bit. I could get hold of someone at DOC and get them to take the supplies next time they go to do maintenance on the hut.'

The disappointment that the prospect of another night in the wilderness with Tom had just vanished was powerful enough to slow Claire's steps. Then she took a deep breath and increased her pace to catch up with Tom again. She'd just remembered something else.

Something she'd told Tom when they were

sharing that first glass of wine and getting to know each other. She'd told him what her new hobby was, hadn't she?

'Making the most of every adventure that comes my way. And if it doesn't come my way, I'll go out and find it...'

Adventures didn't have to be going to a particular place or doing something amazing. Her time with Tom was an adventure and if she didn't make the most of it, she might regret it for the rest of her life.

'Do you know anything about the Marlborough Garden Festival?' she asked as she lengthened her stride to walk by Tom's side. 'Mabel Jamieson told me that I shouldn't miss it while I'm here. And that I really should have a whole weekend in Blenheim and go on as many of the tours as I can.'

'People have been telling me that for years,' Tom said. 'They've given up now, probably because they think I'm not interested in gardens, but it's more that it's not the kind of thing I'd want to do by myself.'

'Like me going into a pub.' Claire looked up to smile at Tom but also to catch her breath before she took what felt like it could be a big step. 'Maybe it's something else we could do together?'

She held his gaze. Tom knew perfectly well that the suggestion was about a lot more than touring beautiful gardens. She'd reassured him that he didn't need to make any confessions to Hanna because this—whatever seemed to be pulling them together again—had a limited shelf life.

Would he think, like her, that it might be something they should make the most of?

The way his gaze was locked on hers felt like that could be exactly what he was thinking.

'Why not?' he said softly as he broke that gaze. 'I love gardens.'

Right from the start it was a weekend that Claire knew she was never going to forget. They booked two full-day tours and the first one let them experience far more than gorgeous manicured gardens. They were lucky enough to get tickets to join a tour that took them out onto the Marlborough Sounds in a boat which had been part of a service that had been running for more than a hundred years, to deliver mail and groceries to remote locations. There were beautiful farm gardens included in the tour but they also got to walk in native forest and along the most stunning beaches Claire had ever seen in her life. The weather was kind, the waters blue and calm and the bonus of a playful pod of dolphins around the boat on the way back to Havelock was almost too perfect.

Claire actually had tears in her eyes as she stood beside Tom on the deck watching the dolphins.

'I don't think I've *ever* been this happy,' she told him.

'I can't believe I've never done this before.' Tom held her gaze for a moment and then bent his head to place a soft kiss on her lips. 'Thank you,' he added.

'What for?'

'This was your idea. I might never have done this, if it wasn't for your adventurous spirit.' He was smiling now. 'You've changed my life, Claire Campbell.'

She hugged those words close as they left the boat, picked up a few supplies in a supermarket in Blenheim and then went to find their accommodation for the night. It was what she'd set out to do when she'd suggested that he kissed her, wasn't it? And when she'd offered to help him rediscover the joy of sex. She'd simply wanted to give Tom more options in his future by restoring his confidence in having a female companion.

She'd had no idea that she might be receiving as much, if not more, than she was giving.

Tom had booked a boutique bed and breakfast location that offered small rustic cottages dotted amongst a leafy vineyard with a backdrop of the dramatic peaks and valleys of the mountains in the distance. The self-catering cottages looked as though they had belonged to early settlers but offered an impressive level of luxury, including a welcoming grazing platter of cheeses, olives and other nibbles, accompanied by a choice of local wines, that was waiting for them on a private veranda so that they could enjoy the sunset and lingering dusk. A few sheep nearby had lambs that were making the most of the last daylight to frolic, which was a delight to watch, and as it started to get darker Claire heard an unexpectedly haunting bird call.

'That sounds like an owl. I didn't know New Zealand had owls.'

'We do. It's the morepork—our only native owl. Its Māori name is ruru, which I believe translates as "big eyes".'

Claire was smiling as she listened to the calls that were being made and answered around them.

'Morepork sounds exactly like the call. As if they're introducing themselves.'

'They could be saying goodnight. We've got another full day's tour tomorrow. Maybe we should get some sleep?'

'Good idea.'

They finally went inside, but as Tom shut the door behind them they caught and held each other's gaze for a long, significant moment as a totally silent conversation played out.

There were two beds in this cottage but they were silently agreeing that they were only going to need one of them and that they might not get as much sleep as they probably should.

And that turned out to be the most perfect part of this garden tour adventure. Claire hadn't been at all bothered by the lumpy old mattress on the floor of that hut the first time she and Tom had been together—that had been perfect in its own way. Perhaps the imperfections of the setting were a reflection of the inevitable hesitations and fumbles of two people who were not only strangers to each other's bodies but hadn't had sex at all for a very long time.

But this was very different. A gorgeously comfortable bed. Two people who had reason to be far more confident and this wasn't their first time with each other. Tom seemed to know exactly where and how to touch Claire that would make her gasp with the pleasure of it and, because she wanted it to be just as good for him, she was remembering everything she could that he had responded to with murmurs of appreciation and she got brave and added to where and how she touched *him* and was rewarded with a groan of ecstasy.

And then they were both lost. It wasn't until Claire was lying in Tom's arms and they were both trying to catch their breath that she realised she'd been wrong earlier. Watching the dolphins hadn't been the moment she'd been the happiest in her entire life.

This was…

It hadn't just been so very different this time because they were getting to know each other's bodies or that the bed was so comfortable. It was because it had been—for her, at least—far more than simply a physical act.

It had been making love…

She was falling in love with Tom Atkinson. Or perhaps it had already happened and it was the bump at the end of the fall that she was feeling now. Maybe she hadn't recognised it for what it was because she'd never experienced it before and it was the last thing she'd expected to find at this time of her life.

She turned her head just a little. Just far enough for her nose and her lips to be against the soft skin under his collarbone. She wanted to soak in the scent and taste and feel of him while she absorbed the realisation of how she was feeling. She wasn't brave enough to say anything. Or maybe she just wanted to keep it secret so there was no chance of Tom reminding her that falling in love again or finding a new partner in life was the last thing he wanted.

It was supposed to be the last thing *she* wanted and maybe, in the cold light of day, she would remember why with more definitive clarity. She would embrace the freedom she'd gifted herself and be grateful that she had the chance to choose exactly where she would go and what she would do to make the most of her life. She would remember what it was like to fall *out* of love and find herself trapped and…diminished. She would never want to risk feeling like that again.

What she did want was the rest of this night, however. She wanted to fall asleep in Tom's arms and dream of a future that could be as perfect as this moment.

CHAPTER NINE

TOM AND CLAIRE had the whole of the next morning to explore acres of a breathtaking classically designed garden in Kekerengu.

They walked along a path of velvety grass, with pointed cypress trees creating a guard of honour on either side. They looked through the round hole under the central arch of a brick wall to the long, thin pond that was still enough to reflect the nearby trees. They wandered through the magic of a pathway with brick pillars and wooden beams overhead, dripping with the long racemes of white wisteria, and they found a wooden bench to sit on and look out to sea when they needed time to let it all sink in.

'I can't believe I've never been here before,' Tom said. 'I've heard about it. I knew it was amazing but I wouldn't be here if it wasn't for you.'

'I would have come on this tour anyway,' Claire admitted. 'But it's so much better being able to share it with someone.'

'That's so true.' Tom nodded slowly. 'You know... I'm beginning to think that Hanna was right in giving me a push. Maybe I do want to find someone to share my life with. To grow old with.' He gave a huff of laughter. 'Old*er*, that is.'

'You're still young,' Claire told him. There was a note in her voice that Tom hadn't heard before. 'But maybe Hanna could see something you were ignoring. That you are lonely sometimes?'

'I had forgotten how good it is to share something like this. To just *be* with someone.' Tom touched Claire's hand where it lay on the bench between them. He felt her go very still and then she turned her hand over and linked her fingers with his. 'It's because of you I know it would actually be possible to have a relationship again. You've...' He paused to let his breath out slowly. 'You've quite possibly changed my whole future, Claire.' His lips curled into a smile. 'By giving me that trial run.'

Claire caught his gaze and held it. She took in a deep breath and opened her mouth but then she didn't say anything and Tom couldn't read her expression. She looked nervous...scared, even?

For a moment he didn't understand and then it hit him. She was thinking that he was going to ask her to stop the pretence. To see them being together as a real couple. To stay here. With him.

For ever...

Of course she was worried. She was probably trying to think up a way to tell him kindly that it was the last thing she'd want. She wasn't going to give up her dreams and her hard-won freedom to chase them. To do exactly what she wanted to do so that she could make the most of the rest of her life and not be held back by the anchor of someone who didn't have the same dreams.

'I'm not as adventurous as you,' he added quickly. 'I admire you so much for having the courage to go and live life exactly the way you want to and I can't wait to hear about all the new and exciting adventures you're going to have.' He shook his head. 'I'd never be brave enough to just walk away to start a new life. To go hunting for new places to live and people to meet.'

'You're more adventurous than you think,' Claire said quietly. 'I'd never be brave enough to go scuba diving. And why would you want to start a new life, anyway? You have a job you love and family and a home. You have a whole community that you're an important part of. You belong here.'

Claire let go of his hand, standing up as if she wanted a better view of the cliff below them and the sea stretching to the horizon.

'It's an incredible place to belong,' she added. 'And you don't have to leave your life behind if you want to meet new people. Maybe Hanna wasn't completely wrong about the online dating. Who knows—you might find someone that would love to go scuba diving with you. Someone your own age, perhaps, so you can grow older at the same rate. Or stay young together for longer.'

Tom blinked. What on earth was Claire talking about? Oh…was she trying to remind him that she was a few years older than him? Why would that make a difference?

Her voice sounded different but he couldn't figure out why. She didn't sound relieved that he'd let her know he wasn't going to ask for anything more than she'd already given him. It was more strained than that. Maybe embarrassed was closer to the truth. She was probably wishing he hadn't started this conversation. He was beginning to wish that himself.

He got to his feet as well. 'Anyway,' he said. 'It's almost time for us to go and have that lunch down the hill at the café. It's included in the tour, isn't it?'

'It is.' Claire did sound relieved as she started moving. 'And I don't know about you, but after all this walking and a bit of sea air, I'm *starving*.'

It wasn't true.

Claire had actually lost her appetite completely. She almost felt a bit sick, in fact.

She'd come so close to telling Tom that she

felt the same way about how good it was to be sharing parts of her life with him. That she was changing her mind about travelling the world in search of new adventures.

Thank goodness she hadn't said anything before he made it so clear that she wasn't the person he wanted to share *his* life with. He didn't want anything more than friendship. To stay in touch and hear about what she was doing in whatever part of the world she moved on to.

That had been her plan so maybe she just needed to get back on track. There were so many other parts of New Zealand she'd love to see, like Central Otago and the North Island. Australia was practically next door, with its vibrant cities and astonishingly vast spaces like the Outback. And what about all those Pacific Islands? She could go and spend as much time as she wanted in a tropical paradise.

It should be such an exciting prospect.

And it would be. She just needed to pretend she was still perfectly happy with her original plan until she could embrace it properly again.

When they arrived at the café she joined the queue where the tour group was invited to help themselves from an impressive buffet of seafood and meat and a huge variety of salads and fresh bread. Tom was just ahead of her, talking to an older woman and her husband about the garden they'd just visited.

'I'm so inspired,' she heard the woman saying. 'I'm going to go home and do something gorgeous with my own garden. Bob will help, won't you, darling?'

Her husband feigned resignation with a sigh. 'I'd better start warming up now,' he said. 'If I know Janice, I'm going to be on the end of a spade as soon as we get home. Or building brick walls or something.'

Claire picked up a serving spoon on top of a huge bowl of Greek salad. If anything was going to tempt her to eat, it would be this mix of tomatoes, cucumber, olives and feta cheese. She didn't get as far as putting any on her plate, however. The sound of a plate shattering as it hit the tiled floor made her turn sharply—just in time to see the woman in front of Tom crumpling as she collapsed against her husband and then slid to the floor.

'Janice!' Bob's cry was panicked. 'Oh, my God...what's happening?'

'Janice?' Tom was shaking the woman's shoulder. 'Can you hear me?'

There was no response.

Tom turned her onto her back. He tilted her head to open the airway and then bent over her, the fingers of one hand on her neck, feeling for a carotid pulse, and his other hand resting on her diaphragm as he watched and felt for any signs of breathing. Claire was beside him as he looked up.

'No pulse, no breathing,' he said. 'Cardiac arrest. Call an ambulance, please, Claire. I think they may have an AED here so grab that, too.'

She nodded, pulling out her phone as she moved to meet the staff members coming towards the commotion. She could see Tom positioning his hands on the woman's chest, starting compressions. He was talking to her terrified-looking husband at the same time.

'Janice's heart has stopped,' he told him. 'Doing CPR will keep her blood moving until we can do more to help her. Does she have any history of heart problems?'

'Yes...' Bob's voice was choked. 'She's had angina for a couple of years now. Not badly. The pain goes away if she has a rest and some of her spray.'

Claire's phone call to the emergency services was swift. An ambulance was being dispatched from Kaikōura and a rescue helicopter would also be dispatched as soon as one was available. Café staff were lifting the buffet tables out of the way and encouraging everybody to move away from the emergency to create space. The manager got the AED from the cabinet on the wall and immediately handed it to Claire.

'I've never used it,' he said. He was looking very pale. 'I'm so glad you guys are here. I've done a first aid course but it's completely different when it's for real, isn't it?'

'You'll be surprised how easy it is,' she told him. 'Just watch and you'll be ready if there's ever a next time. Good for you on having one available—it could well be what saves her life.'

She knelt opposite Tom, who paused his compressions to help her cut the woman's clothing free so that the sticky pads could be attached to bare skin on her upper right chest and lower left side and the heart rhythm could be analysed to determine whether it was appropriate to provide a shock.

They didn't need the instructions the automatic device was giving them but they were loud enough to almost echo in the shocked silence inside the café.

'Call for help now.'
'Apply the pad exactly as shown in the picture.'
'Evaluating heart rhythm. Stop compressions.'
'Shock required. Stand back. Do not touch the patient.'

Claire wriggled her knees further back and Tom held out his arms. 'Stay clear,' he warned.

'Shock delivered. Provide chest compressions.'

Two minutes later they stopped compressions for another rhythm check. Another shock was delivered. But this time, just as Claire was about to take over the next two minutes of compressions, Tom held up his hand.

'Stop! Look...she's moving.'

Claire was holding *her* breath as she watched Janice's mouth open and her chest rise and then fall. Bob had one hand pressed to his mouth and the other was gripping his wife's hand.

'It's all right, Jan,' he said. 'It's going to be all right. You're alive...' He had tears streaming down his face but he was still as white as a sheet. He looked up at Tom. 'She *is* going to be all right, isn't she?'

Tom had his fingers on Janice's wrist. 'She's got a palpable pulse, which means that her heart's working again. We're going to put her into a comfortable position and watch her very carefully until the ambulance gets here. Then we'll be able to do more tests and we'll have everything we need to take the best care of her.'

Janice groaned as Claire helped Tom move her into the recovery position. One of the café staff grabbed a cushion and then a blanket from the shop area. It was one of the blankets with the cute little sheep woven into them that Claire had admired the last time she'd been here.

Janice was semi-conscious by the time the ambulance arrived.

'Where am I?' she asked. 'What happened?'

They put her in the back of the ambulance and worked with the crew to get an IV line established, take a twelve-lead ECG and a full set of vital signs.

'Look at this.' Tom showed Claire the record of the ECG that the life-pack had produced.

'STEMI,' Claire murmured. The elevation of ST segment on the trace was high enough to make the next wave look like small mountains. It was more than enough evidence that Janice was suffering a heart attack that had caused the cardiac arrest. She needed to get to a hospital that could perform angioplasty as quickly as possible.

'I'll travel with her,' Tom told Claire after making another call to the emergency services. 'I've transmitted the ECG to the cardiology department and they'll have a catheter lab on standby for when we arrive. The helicopter's going to meet us at Kaikōura and take her through to Christchurch. Claire, can you drive my car back?'

'No problem.'

'Can I go with Jan too?' Bob begged. *'Please?'*

'Of course you can,' Tom said. 'She needs you right by her side and that's exactly where *you* need to be.'

The expression on his face told Claire that he understood exactly how this man felt, having watched his wife die and then be brought back to life. She caught his gaze as the back doors of the ambulance were being closed and her heart suddenly felt so full it hurt.

So full of love.

She loved everything about Tom. His skill, his compassion, his ability to love. He deserved to find every happiness possible for the rest of his life. It shouldn't feel heartbreaking that it wouldn't be with her because she'd been so sure that it wasn't what *she* wanted for the rest of her life but...

...but maybe she'd been wrong. And it wasn't simply that she loved Tom. She was *in* love with him.

Should she tell Tom that?

Would it change anything?

Claire went back inside, where the staff were doing their best to restore normality and look after their guests. They were all due to move on to the afternoon tour of another garden as soon as they'd had their lunch but Claire decided not to join them. Nothing could beat the last garden she'd seen—with Tom—and she wanted that to be the one she remembered in years to come.

She would go and sit on the beach for a while and be grateful that she was alive and that she'd rediscovered how amazing it was to fall in love with someone. And then she'd drive back to Kaikōura.

Back home.

But first, she'd go and buy one of the sheep blankets. Because it would remind her of...well, everything.

Of the first time they'd come here for lunch.

Of the lambs near the cottage they'd stayed in last night. Where they'd made love and it had been everything she'd ever dreamed it could be.

Of helping Tom save a woman's life and the genuine connection he'd felt with her husband.

Most of all, it would remind her of Tom.

She picked up one of the folded blankets that was tied with a braid of unspun wool. She held it to her cheek for a moment before taking it to the counter. It was soft and warm and she would be able to wrap it around herself and remember it all.

It might even give her the courage to tell Tom that she'd changed her mind. That she didn't want to stay single and travel the world seeking exciting things to do. That maybe she'd found what she was really looking for, without even knowing that she was looking for it.

When Claire took Tom's car back to the Seaview Hospital she was told that he'd ended up going to Christchurch on the helicopter with Janice and Bob. She left his car keys with the senior nurse on duty and walked home, carrying her overnight bag and the sheep blanket.

She draped the blanket over the back of the couch later that day and was standing there admiring it when her phone rang.

'Hey... Tom. Where are you?'

'I just got home after getting a bus back from Christchurch. Thanks so much for bringing my car home.'

'It was no problem at all. Thanks for coming to the garden festival with me.'

'That was absolutely my pleasure. Did you get to the last garden we had booked?'

'No. I didn't think I would have been able to relax enough to enjoy it. How's Janice?'

'Discharged. Good as new. Better than she'd been for some time, anyway.'

'What?' Claire sank onto the sofa. 'She's been discharged already? I thought her ECG showed that she was having a massive anterior infarct. Isn't that the one that's so likely to be fatal it's called the "widow-maker"?'

'I know. Amazing, isn't it? I was invited to observe in the catheter laboratory. I've sent so many patients to get stents but I've never actually seen it done. I think both Bob and Janice were happy that she was going to have someone that wasn't a total stranger in there with her and I was more than happy to stay.'

Tom sounded like he was still buzzing from

the experience. Claire curled her legs beneath her. 'Tell me about it.'

'It was so slick. We landed on the roof of the hospital and went straight to the emergency department and the cath lab was all ready by the time Janice was seen by the cardiology registrar and another ECG and blood tests were taken. It was amazing, Claire. They put the catheter into the radial artery in her wrist and—'

'Her wrist?' Claire interrupted. 'I thought they put it in the femoral artery in the groin. Why the wrist?'

'Much easier to find,' Tom told her. 'And easier to manage after the procedure. You have to keep pressure on a femoral puncture manually for about thirty minutes and then patients have to lie still for up to six hours. They've got a band that can go around the wrist like a mini blood pressure cuff and it gets pumped up and stays there for a couple of hours and then the patient can go home. Bob and Janice were planning to stay in Christchurch overnight because they felt safer staying close to the hospital, just in case. They'll hire a car to get home again tomorrow.'

'Wow... I guess the procedure was successful, then?'

'Textbook,' Tom confirmed. 'They put the catheter in and injected dye and you could see on the X-ray screen exactly where the artery was pretty much a hundred percent blocked—like a dead-end road. The stent got placed and then the balloon was inflated to open it and there it was. You could see the blood flow looking perfectly normal again. Did you know about the drug-eluting stents they can use? They slowly release drugs that can prevent the narrowing that happens after implantation sometimes.'

Claire could hear Tom's breath being released in a sigh. 'It's been quite a day.'

'It was good you were there,' she said. 'Poor Bob looked terrified when he knew that Janice was having a heart attack.'

'Yeah...' There was a note in Tom's voice that told Claire she'd been right in thinking that he had more than empathised with Bob's fear at that point. That he had been remembering the devastation of losing his own wife. 'And...there's something else I should tell you.'

'Oh...?' Claire's heart skipped a beat. Had being with someone who was afraid of losing their life partner made Tom realise what was missing from his life? Had he been thinking about *her* in a different way? Was he going to tell her that he wanted her in his life even before she could tell him how she was feeling about *him*?

'I had a long text conversation with Hanna on the bus trip home,' Tom said. 'I told her the truth.

About the fake dating. I didn't want her to be getting her hopes up too much.'

It felt like Claire's heart stopped for a moment then.

'She's coming for another visit before too long,' Tom added, 'and…what happened today was a sobering reminder that life can be too short. I don't want to be dishonest, even if it's not outright lying. About anything. With any*one*—but especially not with the people I love.'

'I understand,' Claire said quietly. 'Was she upset?'

'She was a bit shocked that people our age would behave like that, but in the end she thought it was funny. She said it would be our secret and she wouldn't tell Kerry so it didn't get around, which might be embarrassing for both of us. She reckoned that it might be better if people just assumed that we didn't want to take it any further. She also said that maybe, one day, I'll listen to her advice about the online dating, but I have my doubts about that. And I'm not going to even think about any kind of dating while you're in town, Claire. I enjoy your company too much.'

There was a tiny pause, as if Tom was taking the time to choose his words carefully.

'I hope we'll always be good friends,' he said. 'No matter where you end up in the world.'

Her voice was even quieter this time. 'I hope so, too.'

Claire stayed on the couch after the call ended. She pulled the sheep blanket down and wrapped it around herself because she needed the touch of something warm and cuddly to comfort her.

She felt as if a door had been slammed in her face. Or maybe it was in her heart.

A dream that had only just formed had just evaporated.

The idea of her finding a fairytale romance at her age was, indeed, ridiculous.

But this didn't have to be a big deal, did it? She had, after all, known that all along, hadn't she?

CHAPTER TEN

THERE WAS NO reason for Tom and Claire to be seen out together now.

No reason to take photographs to be sent to Hanna in order to keep up the pretence that they were dating. They could still go for walks on the beach together or share a meal or a drink together. They could probably still spend the night together, like people did with those friendships that came with 'benefits'. But in the wake of Tom telling Hanna the truth, something had changed.

It felt like they had both taken a step, not backwards—because they knew each other so well now—but sideways. The connection was still there, but there was a bigger gap between them. It felt like an elastic gap, as if it could change in either direction, and sometimes Claire got the impression that Tom would like to make it smaller. It felt like he was missing that intimate time they'd had together.

Claire was certainly missing it, but the kind of courage needed to chase an adventure she'd particularly wanted that had led to her inviting Tom to go to the garden festival with her was nowhere to be found now. She wasn't about to make things any harder for herself by getting that close to Tom again. She only had to remember him telling her that he hoped they would remain friends no matter where she was in the world to stop herself saying, or doing, anything that might reveal how she felt about him.

Because...if Tom had felt anything like that himself, he wouldn't have bothered telling Hanna the truth about the fake dating, would he? How it had all begun could have been *their* secret if it had morphed into a real relationship and telling Hanna later really would have made it funny. The kind of funny story that got told at weddings?

Oh, *help*...where had that thought come from? Claire had been confident that she was getting past the discomfort of having let herself get in too deep. She was focusing on work and getting more involved with her new community by joining a book club and a yoga class. She was keeping an eye out for any interesting nursing positions that were being advertised. Not that she wanted to leave Kaikōura any time soon, but if she couldn't get perfectly comfortable with the idea of nothing more than a friendship with Tom, it might become wise to move on. What if he did take Hanna's advice to start dating? Or he might decide he wanted to but was trapped by having said he wouldn't while Claire was still in town.

She still had more than half the lease of her little cottage left, however. There was no rush, was there?

Claire loved it here.

She really didn't want to be anywhere else.

The patients she saw on a regular basis, especially the ones she visited in their homes, were becoming an important part of her life. Mabel Jamieson was a delight and now that her granddaughter, Olivia, was home from hospital after the surgery on her oesophageal cancer, Mabel was determined to be as involved as everyone else in the family to provide the core of the wraparound support that the whole community was wanting to contribute to.

She was there when Claire made her first home visit, sitting in a big armchair in the corner of Olivia's bedroom, reading a story to Lucy, who was sitting on her lap. Yvonne was perched on the end of her daughter's bed.

'How are you feeling, Liv?' Claire asked.

'It's good to be home. But I'm *so* tired. I can't get out of bed for more than a few minutes at a time.'

'You've been through major surgery,' Claire reminded her. 'It's going to take time, but it will get easier.' She checked Olivia's temperature and heart rate and how the skin around her surgical wounds was looking, happy to record that there was no sign of infection. 'Try and get up as often as you feel up to it,' she said. 'And go outside, even if it's just for a minute. A bit of sunshine and fresh air can be a real boost.'

'Lucy's desperate to show her the sunflower plants we put in while Liv was in hospital,' Yvonne said. 'She thinks they're nearly as big as she is.'

Olivia's smile looked like an effort. 'I'll try later, Mum.'

'How's the eating going?' Claire asked. 'Dr Atkinson said you were finding it a bit difficult when he saw you yesterday.'

'It hurts to swallow. He's given me some new painkillers and something for the reflux that he thinks might help.'

'You know to try and eat small amounts often and stay sitting up for an hour or so after eating?'

'Yeah...and I can only eat baby food mush for the next six weeks.'

'It can be tasty, though.' Claire put a waterproof cloth on the side of the bed and started to collect what she needed for today's visit, which was to remove Olivia's stitches. 'What's your favourite meal?'

Yvonne responded when Olivia simply shrugged. 'She's always requested roast chicken for any special meals like birthdays. With lots of potatoes and gravy.'

'There you go.' Claire smiled. 'You can make that and put it in the blender until it's the consistency of mashed potatoes. It might feel like baby food but the flavours should still be there.' She touched Olivia's hand. 'It *will* get better,' she said gently. 'But, like the shampoo ads, it won't happen overnight.'

Olivia's small smile felt like a win.

'Now…let's get these stitches out, shall we?'

The surgery had involved incisions in her abdomen, the side of her chest and in her neck. Claire took the dressings off each site and cleaned the wounds with an antiseptic swab. She held the knot of each stitch in tweezers, pulling it up far enough to snip the suture beneath the knot with her sterile scissors. Then she pulled the stitch out gently and laid it on a gauze square to check that it was intact.

Yvonne stayed on the end of the bed, rubbing Olivia's leg occasionally in support. They could all hear the soothing sound of Mabel in the background, reading a story that Lucy clearly loved because she was able to join in every sentence with her great-grandmother. It made Olivia smile every time she heard her daughter's voice as she lay back against her pillows, with her eyes closed. Claire didn't want to interrupt something that was providing comfort so she stayed quiet as she got on with what was an easy, automatic task.

She knew Tom had been in to visit the family yesterday, when Olivia had arrived home, and plans had been made for her to start her chemotherapy sessions in a few weeks' time. They could be done in Seaview Hospital and would only happen once a week in three-week cycles. A central venous line had been inserted to provide painless IV access and it would be one of Claire's duties to watch for any signs of infection around that site on her upcoming visits. She would also be providing whatever other support she could in her role as a community nurse. For Olivia. And Mabel, who needed a dressing change on her ulcers today as well.

The gauze square was almost covered with the tiny black threads of the sutures. Claire would be able to clean the wounds again when all the stitches were out and then apply some sticky strips to protect the skin from tension as it continued to heal.

She wanted to be here to see more than just these wounds heal, Claire realised. She wanted to be here as part of the support team for the whole Jamieson family—as Tom would be. Olivia had been one of his first patients when he'd started his career as a doctor. He had probably delivered her daughter, Lucy. He would be here to share the sadness when the family had to say goodbye to Mabel and, even if he was retired, he would still be here to share the joy of Lucy growing up and maybe starting her own family.

How wonderful would it be to belong somewhere like that?

It would be far more fulfilling than moving from place to place, searching for…what? A fleeting experience that could qualify as an adventure? A place or activity that would bring pleasure?

That wasn't what Claire wanted at all.

She wanted to belong, too.

Not necessarily to a single person. Maybe a place would be enough. Somewhere beautiful—like here. Or a community, where she could build connections to people—like Mabel and Olivia and Carl and…yes…to Tom and Hanna.

She wanted to feel needed. *Wanted*, even.

To know that she *was* good enough.

'Are you okay, Dad?'

'I'm fine, Hanna. More than fine. I'm delighted that you've managed to squeeze in a couple of days to come home.'

'Hmm…' Hanna didn't sound convinced. 'You just don't seem as happy as you were the last time I was here.'

'I am at work. I'll be my usual happy self when

I get home later. Want me to bring some fish and chips home for dinner?'

'No, I'll make something. I'm going to catch up with Kerry and then I'll do a supermarket run. Is there anything you want me to pick up for you?'

'I forgot to get any oat milk in for you, I'm sorry.'

'No problem. Anything you'd like for a treat? Your favourite ice cream, maybe?'

Tom shook his head. 'I'm good.'

But Hanna was giving him a thoughtful look. 'I heard about Livvy Jamieson,' she said quietly. 'And I know how involved you always get with your patients.'

Tom shuffled some papers on his desk. 'It's not easy,' he agreed. 'But it's a privilege to be part of looking after her—and the family.'

'You've got to look after yourself, too, Dad.' Hanna frowned. 'And get some time away from work. Have you been out with Pete for a dive?'

'Not for a while. We've both been busy.'

'Have you and Claire gone out lately? For dinner, or a movie or something?'

Tom shook his head. 'I told you we were never really dating, remember?'

'You also told me that you'll always be great friends. Friends get to spend time together. They get to make each other feel better if they're having a tough time.' Hanna got to her feet. 'I'll get out of your way and let you get on with work. We'll have plenty of time to talk later.'

She walked around the desk to plant a kiss on her father's cheek. 'And I've changed my mind. Fish and chips for dinner is exactly what I feel like.'

Tom finished clearing his desk in preparation for the afternoon clinic hours. He wasn't surprised that Hanna had noticed he didn't seem as happy as the last time she'd been here.

He *wasn't* as happy. And it wasn't simply because he was worried about some of his patients, like Livvy. He was missing spending time with Claire but could that be fixed by simply going out for a coffee or a movie with her, as a friend? Tom was hesitant to even suggest it, in fact, now that Hanna knew they weren't actually dating. Neither could he forget that look on Claire's face when she'd thought he was about to say that she was the person he'd like to share his life with.

And if she was missing spending time with him, as a friend, she'd suggest something, wouldn't she? She'd been the one to suggest that he went on the garden tour with her, after all.

With a sigh, Tom got to his feet and headed towards Reception so he could pick up a set of notes and call for the person who had the first appointment this afternoon. If his path crossed with Claire's he knew they would both smile and, to all outward appearances, nothing had changed. He knew better, however. He just wished he knew how to fix the odd tension that was between them. Maybe having Hanna here for a visit would make a difference. The weather was looking settled for the next few days so perhaps they could put on a barbecue at home. She could invite all her friends and he could invite his.

Including Claire.

Especially Claire.

The barbecue was a great idea. There was a real hint of approaching summer and the weather was warm enough for the group of Seaview medical staff, family and friends to be enjoying the Atkinsons' garden and the aroma of the meat and seafood cooking on the grill. Tom had been out with his mate, Pete, and there were crayfish and snapper on the menu, along with the ubiquitous sausages and steak.

Best of all, there didn't seem to be any awkwardness when Claire met Hanna again as she went inside to add her contribution of a dessert to the shared meal. She got a warm hug from Tom's daughter and then a wink.

'Your secret's safe with me,' she said. 'I did tell Kerry that you're not an item any longer but I didn't say why. And I said that you're still good friends.'

'We are,' Claire said. 'He's a lovely man, your dad. I must go and meet Pete properly. I've heard a lot about him.'

She enjoyed a glass of wine as she was introduced to Pete and chatted with her colleagues and met their partners. She stood by Tom for a while as he basted the crayfish tails with garlic and butter. She could still feel the hum between them. The warmth in Tom's eyes as he smiled at her suggested that he could feel it too and Claire decided it would only take a nudge for one of them to step over that invisible line and say something that would make that gap between them shrink enough to vanish.

Just a small nudge would do the trick. Like arranging to meet for a coffee and a walk on their next shared day off.

'Could you find Hanna and let her know we'll be ready in a few minutes?' Tom asked. 'She and Kerry went inside to sort the salads, I think.'

'Sure.'

Hanna *was* in the kitchen with her friend Kerry but they weren't doing anything with the salads. They were both peering at Hanna's phone.

'Ah... Claire... Just the person we need.'

'Oh...?'

'Yes.' Hanna bit her lip. 'Don't tell Dad about this, will you?'

'About what?'

'Well... I didn't exactly delete that profile I made for him on that dating site. I just snoozed it.'

Her smile was a mix of being apologetic and conspiratorial. 'I think he's feeling lonely now that you two aren't spending so much time together so Kerry and I were just looking at the profiles of all the women that sent him kisses in the first place to see if we can choose someone. You're probably a better judge than we are about who he might fancy.'

Claire blinked. Really? They wanted her to help choose a potential partner for Tom to share his life with? Someone that he would be *attracted* to? It was the last thing she wanted to do but it was too late. The girls were on either side of her now and Hanna's phone was in front of her.

'Look... This Penelope is rather gorgeous, isn't she?'

'Mmm...' Claire tried to keep her tone neutral. 'But how old is she?'

'Forty-five. That's only nine years younger than Dad and he doesn't really look his age, does he?'

'No.' Claire had to agree. 'I would have guessed he was in his late forties when I met him.'

'I like that one...' Kerry said. 'Jasmine. She's got a cute dog.'

Jasmine also looked to be in her early forties.

Young enough to be Claire's daughter, in fact. Definitely young enough to remind her of the person her husband was now happily sharing his life with.

Tom would have no problem attracting someone like Penelope or Jasmine or any of the dozens of hopeful women on this dating site. Thanks to Claire, he wouldn't have any misgivings about knowing where to start in getting to know them.

He should have all the confidence he needed to kiss them.

And that would, no doubt, inevitably lead to—

Thank goodness her thoughts were abruptly unable to go any further in that direction because Tom had just walked into the kitchen. Hanna hastily shoved her phone into the back pocket of her jeans and Claire held her breath, hoping that it wasn't obvious they'd been talking about him.

Hoping even more that her own thoughts were completely invisible.

Tom didn't seem at all perturbed.

'Where have those salads got to?' he asked. 'There's a hungry crowd out there.'

It was in the evening when she was alone at home, nearly a week later, that Claire received a text message from a number she didn't recognise.

Hey, Claire. Hanna here. Dad gave me your number. Hope you don't mind?

Claire sent a message back.

Not at all. How are you?

She got a smiley face emoji in return. And a short plea.

I need your help.

Is this about your dad?

Yes. I think I've found someone for him. She even lives in Kaikōura and loves scuba diving!! He's never going to agree to a blind date but I have a plan. I've given it a code name. Happy Ever After.

The emoji was a winking face this time. Closely followed by a pair of crossed fingers.
Claire could feel a chill run down her spine as she tapped the letters on her phone.

And it involves me?

You are the only way it could work. Are you up for it?

Was she? Did Claire want Tom to live happily ever after?

Of course she did.

With another woman?

Well…it would have to be, wouldn't it? Because it wasn't going to be with her.

She texted back.

I need more info. Give me five minutes to make a cup of tea and call me?

The response pinged in instantly—a 'thumbs up' emoji.

CHAPTER ELEVEN

THE PLAN WAS SIMPLE.

On their next shared day off, Claire would text Tom and suggest meeting for a coffee at one of the trendy cafés in town.

Tom would arrive at the café and sit down to wait for her but Claire was going to be late. She was, in fact, not going to turn up at all.

'You'll think of a reason,' Hanna assured her. 'Maybe you get a phone call from the UK, or an old lady falls over in the street and needs your medical expertise? You can text him to say sorry, but you can't make it.'

The woman who wanted to meet him—Lorraine, her name was—would be in the café as well. When Claire failed to show up, she would use the opportunity to strike up a conversation with Tom.

'It might well come to nothing,' Hanna admitted. 'But at least it's a way of getting him to say hello to someone, isn't it? And who knows? They might really like each other.'

Claire hadn't felt great about the plan but Hanna had been very persuasive and she'd promised to think about it. A sleepless night led her to the conclusion that, while Tom had thought her new motto in life of everything being all about herself from now on was brilliant and brave, she'd been the one who'd raised the real truth of the matter.

How incredibly selfish would it be to stand in the way of Tom's happiness to spare her own feelings?

She regretted her decision to play her part in the scheme a few days later, however, the moment she received Tom's text saying he'd love to meet for coffee and suggesting that they went for a walk on the beach afterwards. When the time came that she had arranged to meet Tom in the café and she was supposed to simply leave him waiting alone and then send a message to say she wasn't going to come after all, it was suddenly overwhelmingly unacceptable to have been so deceptive. This wasn't about her. It was about Tom's integrity and need for honesty in his life.

The cottage door banged shut behind her as she left a short time later. Maybe she could catch up with Tom before he got there and let him know that his daughter was up to a bit of mischief again. What she couldn't do was stand him up and then make up a story as an excuse. He deserved better than that from both her and Hanna. He deserved to know the truth, not just about being set up on a blind date but how she felt about him. It might make absolutely no difference at all but Claire wouldn't have to spend the rest of her life regretting that she hadn't found the courage to do that.

She had to pause as she reached the beach, to find her sunglasses in her bag. Life in London had not prepared her for how bright the light could be here. It felt like summer today and the sun seemed to be reflecting off a sea that was the calmest she'd ever seen it. Claire increased her pace after that but she didn't get to the café in time to intercept Tom.

He was already there. She paused again, waiting to cross to the other side of the street, and she could see him sitting at one of the outside tables. She saw the woman who casually sat down at the next table but turned almost immediately to talk to Tom. It had to be Lorraine and it only took a heartbeat for Claire to get a first impression. The star of this setup was wearing tight jeans that were rolled up to her calves and a tee shirt that showed off the rest of her gorgeous figure. She had sun-streaked blonde hair and a wide smile and…and she looked even younger than the profile pictures that had caught Hanna's attention on the night of the barbecue.

What was worse, however, was that Claire could see that it was Tom's attention that was firmly caught right now as he smiled and said something back to the stranger.

Her feet felt stuck to the footpath. There was no way she could walk over the road and interrupt them. For all she knew, this might be Tom's first conversation with the woman he was going to spend the rest of his life with.

Claire swallowed hard and then pulled out her phone before she could change her mind.

I can't make it after all. So sorry.

She stayed where she was for a moment, watching Tom read the text message. Even from this distance she could see him frown but then he turned as Lorraine said something else to him. And then, as smoothly as if she'd rehearsed her part in this charade, she saw the beautiful, *young* woman get up and move to sit at Tom's table.

That was when Claire felt the prickle of tears and the shaft of something painful that felt like a piece breaking off her heart. That was when she turned and started walking back the way she'd come. She was grateful for the sunglasses for more than the protection from bright light now. Nobody was likely to recognise her and, even if they did, they wouldn't be able to see how upset she was.

But, disconcertingly, she could hear someone calling her name.

'*Claire*... Wait up...'

She had to turn her head to glance over her shoulder. And then she had to stop.

'Carl!' It was impossible not to respond to the cheerful grin the boat skipper was giving her. 'How are you?'

He waved his hand at her. 'I've ditched the glove. Look... Almost as good as new.'

'That's great, Carl.' She noted the watertight latex dressing over the tip of the finger. 'Good to see you're still looking after your scar.'

'Keeping it covered reminds me to be careful. It hurts if I put too much pressure on it and I don't want to cause any more damage but...' Carl shook his head, talking fast '...that's not what I wanted to talk to you about. There's been a sighting of a giant sperm whale earlier today. The conditions are perfect and I'm taking my boat out right now. There's one space left on it and I knew as soon as I spotted you that it's got your name on it. Are you up for it?'

Oh... Those were the exact words Hanna had used when she'd wanted Claire to help her set her dad up on a date. Claire couldn't help looking past Carl to where she could still see Tom. Still sitting with Lorraine. A staff member was standing beside the table now, with a notepad in her hand, clearly taking their orders for coffee and maybe one of the cookies the café was known for.

That did it.

Claire had been promising herself the treat of going out whale watching ever since she'd arrived in this town. Maybe it was time to return to Plan A and make life all about herself again. But first, she had to get over this ridiculous pain of losing something—a future with Tom Atkinson—that had only ever existed in her imagination and Carl, bless him, had just offered her the perfect first step.

'I'm so up for it,' she told him.

The catamaran had two powerful outboard motors, a cabin that contained indoor seating, a table and the skipper's cockpit and an outside area with padded bench seats on either side and a solid canopy for shelter. Lifejackets had been provided for the passengers and there was a sound system so everybody could hear the snippets of information Carl was telling them as they sped away from the wharf. He congratulated people on choosing such an awesome day to go whale watching, talked about the different varieties of whales they might be lucky enough to encounter and threw in some housekeeping rules for safety, when afternoon tea would be served and that there was a toilet available down a step near the front of the boat. Claire was particularly pleased to hear that but, despite the calm sea, she didn't want to try moving around the boat while they were travelling at speed.

By the time they slowed down, she'd forgotten about wanting to go to the toilet. While everyone else, including Carl, who was using a pair of binoculars, looked out to sea to try and spot a whale's tail or a spout of water, she was looking behind the boat, where the township of Kaikōura nestled under the mountains across a stretch of impossibly blue sea.

How lucky was she to have discovered this tiny, astonishing patch of the world. She loved it. She felt happier here than she ever had in London.

Tom was somewhere in the middle of that idyllic scene, she thought.

Was that why it felt so much like home?

A call from someone made her turn her head. People were shading their eyes as they peered over the open sides of the boat. Inside, Carl was holding his binoculars in place with one hand. With the other, he reached for his microphone.

'That, my friends,' he said, 'looks to me like the blow of a blue whale. They're baleen whales, like humpbacks, which means they have two blowholes, but the blue's the only one that can send a cloud of water high enough to hang in the air like that, even after the whale's made its dive. We'll head in that direction and see if we're going to be lucky enough to get another glimpse.'

There was an air of excited anticipation amongst the passengers now that only grew as Carl kept the speed of the boat much lower. He even lowered his voice as he spoke—as if this was a momentous occasion.

'We do get blue whales in these parts all year round,' he told them, 'but spotting them is pretty special. They were hunted almost to extinction in the nineteen-thirties and they tend to be solitary creatures unless it's mating season.'

Claire was fascinated now. She leaned over the rail at the back of the boat, trying to spot another cloud of whale breath.

'They're the biggest—and loudest—animals on the planet,' Carl said. 'Their heart weighs about one hundred and eighty kilos. That's two of me, folks. And their tongue weighs as much as an elephant. They can be up to thirty metres long—that's three times as long as this boat.'

There was a collective gasp from the passengers, loud enough to be heard over the engine noise, when the enormous whale broke the surface of the sea not far ahead of the boat. Carl cut the engine and they floated in silence as they watched the head coming further out of the water until the blowholes were clear to expel a huge cloud of moisture into the air. Then its body kept rising before beginning to gently curve as the head went below water. Everybody had their phones out, taking videos or photographs as they waited for the magical moment of the tail coming up until the flukes were the only visible part of the magnificent creature.

And then it vanished below the surface and the white foam of the disturbed sea gradually faded.

'It might breach again,' Carl said. 'I can't start the engine again until I know where it is. Be prepared. It could come up a lot closer to the boat this time.'

They waited, *Time and Tide* rocking gently on the ocean. Another whale watching boat was approaching the area carefully and a helicopter could be seen coming from the shore. Word of the special visitor was obviously spreading. Minutes ticked past and there was still no sign of the whale.

That was when Claire's bladder gave her a much stronger reminder of how full it was so she ducked into the cabin of the boat. Carl was standing between his chair and the steering wheel, screens and dials of his instrument panel, scanning the ocean in front of them. Claire could see the step down on the other side of the boat.

'The loo's down there, yes?'

'Yep. Use the handrail. It's a big step.'

It was a small space, built partly below floor level to make it tall enough to stand up in comfortably, and it had a metal door that shut firmly. Claire was about to unlock the door to let herself out again when it happened.

She felt the impact through the wall of this space as something hit the boat so hard she was thrown against the small basin on the opposite wall. The sound of the impact was followed by the even more horrific sound of people screaming. And then, too fast for Claire to feel frightened, she could feel her feet leaving the floor. She clung to the taps of the basin as her whole body twisted. She lost her grip on the taps and tried to reach the door but she was totally disoriented. She couldn't even *find* the door.

And that was when fear took hold—just as cold and inescapable as the water enveloping her.

Tom read the text message from Claire saying she couldn't make it to the café for coffee again and he could feel his frown deepening. This was so unlike her that he was sure something untoward must have happened, but why hadn't she told him what it was and whether she was okay?

'You on your own?' It wasn't the first time the woman had spoken to him. They'd exchanged a friendly comment about what a lovely day it was when she'd arrived at almost the same time he had and they'd chosen neighbouring tables.

'Apparently so. I was supposed to be meeting a friend for coffee but she can't make it.'

'Oh, no...you've been stood up?' The attractive blonde woman was smiling at him. 'I feel like I'm getting the death glare from people in that queue waiting for a table and I'm on my own as well. Can I join you? That way I might look like a local and not a tourist that's taking up too much space.' She was getting out of her seat and moving to sit on the other side of his small table before Tom had a chance to say anything. 'I'm Lorraine, by the way. And I'm not a tourist. I've just moved here.'

Tom's manners prevented him from ignoring his new companion to focus on his phone enough to send a message. It would have been even more rude to tell the staff member who came to their table with her notepad that he'd changed his mind about having coffee when he was already sitting here. Lorraine had ordered a cappuccino but Tom asked for a simple flat white.

'To have here?' she checked.

Inspiration struck and Tom shook his head. 'To take away, please.'

If it wasn't possible to spend some time with Claire, the next best thing would be to catch up with Pete. He could drive over to the marina where Pete kept the boat he used for any chartered fishing or diving expeditions. If his friend wasn't out with some clients, he would undoubtedly be messing about on his boat.

'Make that two coffees,' he added. 'And throw in a couple of your delicious chocolate chip cookies.' He got to his feet. People didn't usually sit at the tables when they were ordering a takeaway coffee. 'I'll come in with you and wait for them.' He smiled at Lorraine. 'Enjoy your coffee. And welcome to Kaikōura.'

Her smile didn't reach her eyes and Tom suddenly realised that this woman might have been hoping for more than a companion to drink her coffee with. He should be flattered that such an attractive woman had approached him, he thought. But he didn't feel flattered. He felt… uncomfortable. He'd been looking forward to spending some time with Claire. He didn't want to spend that time with another woman. It felt almost as if it would be cheating, but that was ridiculous, wasn't it? They weren't in any kind of relationship.

So why did he find himself thinking about Claire now? Feeling concerned about what had prevented her getting to the café. He should drop in on his way home, he decided. Just to make sure she was okay. He'd pay for Lorraine's coffee as well before he left the café and maybe that small kindness would make her day a little better.

Finding that Pete was on his boat made Tom's day instantly better.

'Want to head out for a spot of fishing?' Pete asked as he finished his coffee. 'I don't have anyone on the books for this afternoon.'

'Why not?' Tom nodded.

They made a plan to head north to Ohau Point and try for some snapper or gurnard, but changed their minds before they rounded the tip of the peninsula, when they heard the chatter on the common VHF radio channel which allowed boats to communicate with each other.

'Sounds like they've spotted a blue whale,' Pete said. 'Want to hang around here instead?'

'Too right,' Tom said. 'That's an opportunity not to be missed. I've never seen a blue.'

Word was clearly spreading. They could see a helicopter taking off from the airport to head towards them and one of the bigger whale watching boats was doing a U-turn from the popular tourist attraction of the local seal colony. An excited voice came over the radio.

'Thar she blows!'

The spout of water was easily big enough to be seen from shore as the massive whale began to surface. But then someone was shouting.

'That's Carl's boat!'

Another voice was on the channel now. A calm voice that was following standard procedure for an emergency.

'*Mayday, mayday, mayday!* Boat *Time and Tide* capsized. Looked like it got swiped by a whale.'

'I can see people in the water,' came another panicked-sounding message.

The Kaikōura coastguard was on the channel now and Tom could hear the siren that summoned their volunteers to man the rescue boat. They wanted to gather more information in the time for them to get the boat down the slipway and on its way but nobody could tell them how many people were in the water, whether there were any injuries or how rapidly the boat might be sinking.

Pete caught Tom's gaze and reached for his microphone and identified himself as he joined the conversation. 'On our way,' he said then. 'I've got a doctor on board. And diving gear. ETA five minutes.'

Two other boats reached the scene at about the same time that Tom and Pete arrived.

They could see the twin hulls of *Time and Tide* just breaking the surface of what was, very fortunately, an unusually calm sea.

'Must be some air pockets inside,' Pete noted,

slowing his boat as they approached. 'That's good news for being able to salvage her.'

Tom wasn't thinking about the boat. There were people in the water and he was very relieved to see they were all wearing life jackets. A child was being lifted into one of the other boats and a woman clung to a lifebuoy that had been thrown from the whale watch vessel. The helicopter was hovering overhead, possibly relaying information to the coastguard, but Tom's attention was caught by a man who wasn't far from the unturned boat and was waving frantically at them. They could hear him shouting.

'Help... This guy needs help!'

Pete took them closer. The man who was shouting was holding onto another man, keeping his head out of the water as he was floating on his back. His face was pale and his eyes were closed. Was he unconscious? Or—

'It's Carl.' Pete swore under his breath. He climbed down the ladder at the back of the boat and hooked one arm around Carl. Tom leaned over the side and managed to get a grip on an arm. The man in the water did his best to help and, with a huge effort, they managed to drag the limp body on board and place him flat on his back.

'Carl...' Tom shook his shoulder. 'Can you hear me? Can you open your eyes?'

The man who'd helped with Carl was clinging to the boat's ladder.

'Was he unconscious when you found him?' Tom queried. 'Face down in the water?'

'No. He was swimming. And coughing like crazy. He didn't want me to hold him—it was like he wanted to get back under the water.'

Tom nodded. He could understand that. *Time and Tide* was Carl's livelihood—almost a family member.

Another boat came alongside them, reaching to take the man on board. He turned before taking their hands.

'And then he passed out. Just a couple of minutes ago.'

'Coastguard's on its way,' the crew told them. 'And the ambulance will be waiting on shore. One of the docs from the hospital will be with them.'

Tom gave a terse nod. He'd heard that message on the radio. He looked up at Pete. 'He's got a faint pulse,' he said. 'But he's not breathing.'

He tilted Carl's head back, pinched his nose, took in a breath and then sealed his lips over Carl's to deliver a slow, steady rescue breath, one hand on his chest to feel for its rise.

One breath. And then another.

He needed to start chest compressions because, with no breathing, it was only a matter of time before Carl went into cardiac arrest. But just as he positioned his hand in the centre of the chest, Carl moved, rolling onto his side and retching before spitting out water.

'It's okay, mate.' Pete's voice sounded wobbly. 'You're going to be okay.'

Carl groaned again, trying to speak, but his words were too hoarse to understand.

'Just take a breath,' Tom told him. 'As deep as you can. And another one...' He was checking Carl's pulse, which was gaining strength. His breathing sounded remarkably clear, too. Maybe it had been laryngospasm that had stopped him breathing and he hadn't ended up with any water in his lungs. He still needed to get to hospital as soon as possible, though. To get dry and warm and to be given oxygen and monitored carefully for potential complications, especially to the lungs, like pneumonia or the development of acute respiratory distress syndrome.

The coastguard boat was beside them now and they were the best crew to get Carl to the waiting ambulance. They needed some information first, however.

'How many passengers were on the boat, Carl? Was it eight?'

'Yeah...' Carl still sounded croaky.

'We've got four men, three women and a kid.'

'Anyone injured?' Tom asked.

'Doesn't seem to be. They're cold and scared.' The coastguard skipper turned back to Carl. 'So it was just you and eight passengers on board? That's all?'

Carl shook his head. '...one extra... Claire...'

Tom could feel himself freeze. *Claire* was on board?

'She was...in the toilet...' Carl was trying to sit up as well as speak. 'Tried to...open the door... Had to...come up for air...'

One of the coastguard crew was getting onto Pete's boat with the scoop stretcher they would use to transfer Carl.

Tom should go with him but he was breathing well now and he'd be with the ambulance crew and another doctor—probably Ian—within just a few minutes.

And...and how could he leave if Claire was trapped beneath that capsized boat?

Oh, dear Lord...

The realisation that he might never see Claire Campbell alive again hit Tom so hard the breath rushed out of his body. For a moment, he wondered if he would ever be able to take another one.

He *had* to see Claire, he realised.

He had to be the one to find her.

And even if she would never be able to hear his words, he had to tell her what he'd realised, beyond any shadow of doubt, in that terrible moment.

That he loved her.

That he needed her in his life. Without Claire, his life was never going to be what it could have been.

What he desperately *wanted* it to be.

CHAPTER TWELVE

IT WAS A friendship that was so longstanding and so close that Pete and Tom could work together with the bare minimum of verbal communication. That meant that they could work fast but, right now, it still felt too slow for Tom.

It had already taken too long to persuade others that he should be the one to put scuba diving gear on and get into the boat below the surface. The coastguard crew had a responsibility to identify and manage the risks involved, like the possibility of losing whatever air pocket could be providing the buoyancy to keep the boat afloat and that *Time and Tide* could start sinking, perhaps suddenly, into what was very deep water out here.

Nobody was saying it out loud, but if this was simply a body retrieval it was unwise to be rushing into anything and risking another life.

'But what if there's an air pocket that's keeping Claire alive?' Tom had to make an effort to keep his voice calm. 'I'm not prepared to lose the limited window of time we might have available. I *am* prepared to take that risk.'

He was more than prepared. He wouldn't be able to live with himself if he didn't.

And Pete was totally on board. Literally.

He had all the diving gear they needed on his boat. He was checking that the air tank was full, attaching the regulators and strapping it into a dive vest as Tom was finally given the green light and got himself into a wetsuit, thick enough to protect him from both the very cold water and any potentially sharp hazards he might encounter in a confined space.

Wetsuits were never quick garments to get into but Tom knew that getting it wet by dunking it into seawater over the side of the boat would make it easier and, more importantly, faster. He stripped down to his boxers and then shoved one leg and then the other in and tugged the suit higher bit by bit, up to his knees and then his waist. Then he put his arms into the sleeves and turned, holding his shoulders back, so that Pete could pull up the zip on the back. He put flippers on. His arms went through the shoulder straps of the vest and Pete helped lift the tank and secure it. Tom didn't want to take the time to find and put on a hood or gloves. He pulled a mask over his eyes and picked up the mouthpiece to settle the flanges in place. He double-checked the tank pressure, took a breath of the air to make sure everything was working as it should and then sat on the edge of the boat, his back to sea.

Pete's hand signal asked if he was okay. Tom nodded. Then Pete held up a hand with his fingers crossed to wish him luck, but his expression made it more like he was offering his mate the strength to get through what might be the worst possibility. Tom didn't acknowledge that he might have to bring Claire's body to the surface. He wasn't going to let anything destroy the hope he was desperately hanging onto. He held his mask and regulator in place with one hand, his other hand on the back of his head as he rolled backwards into the water.

He sank, twisted to turn his body and then headed towards the capsized boat that was easily visible in this clear water. It felt like it took too long to get close enough to touch the rails at the back of the boat. Then he had to pull himself towards the cabin. The cockpit door wasn't completely closed, which made it easier for Tom to pull it open far enough to get inside. Larger pieces of debris had to be cleared so that he could move through the cabin—a fishing tackle box, a first aid kit and a large plastic container that looked as though it was full of supplies for an afternoon tea. He had to avoid hazards, like floating ropes and fishing rods that he didn't want to get tangled in, as he moved towards the skipper's seat, which should have been attached to the floor but was now overhead. The step down to the toilet was now above his head and Tom used the sloping rail near the step to steady himself. His heart was thumping so hard he could hear it as he tried to open the door.

And failed.

He thumped on the door. He couldn't even speak with his mouthpiece in, let alone shout Claire's name aloud, but the thought was loud enough to echo inside his head.

Claire...

The initial panic had stopped spiralling completely out of control when Claire had discovered the air pocket. She was between the base of the toilet and the hand basin and there was a pipe she could hang onto to keep her head in the space that was, miraculously, full of air rather than seawater. She had no idea how she was going to get out but she was alive. Maybe all she needed to do was to hang on and rescue would come.

Except it hadn't come and Claire had lost track of time and it was so dark it felt like the middle of the night and she was getting so cold it was hard to keep her grip on the pipe. She tried shouting for help but knew how unlikely it was that anyone would be able to hear her. She couldn't hear anything from the outside. How far underwater was she? She didn't think the boat had sunk to the ocean floor because it was moving—rocking gently, both up and down and sideways.

As minute after minute ticked past and Claire could feel her toes and then her feet and legs going numb, she knew it was only a matter of time before she wouldn't be able to hang on any longer. Or that she would use up all the oxygen available in this trapped bubble of air and that would be the end. Panic threatened to overwhelm her again but she made a deliberate effort to slow her breathing.

She didn't want to have her last moments alive filled with fear so she did her best to try and focus on the things in her life that had brought her the greatest happiness. While there were things in her past that she would always treasure—like the countless times she'd held her beloved daughter in her arms—what sprang to mind right now, with remarkable clarity as she closed her eyes and turned her thoughts inwards, were far more recent memories.

And they all included Tom Atkinson.

That first hug on the beach when the connection was so powerful it felt unbreakable. They both knew how it felt to try and ride a wave of unbearable grief. They both knew how short life could be and how moments of joy and this kind of connection needed to be treasured.

Seeing the 'smoke' of the Milky Way above the ancient brick chimney. It was a gift that Tom had bestowed on her that would be high on any list of the best moments of Claire's life.

That first kiss would have absolutely made it onto that list, as well.

And the night in the cabin up on the mountain. Right from the start, when they knew they were going to be there alone together all night and Tom was breaking up the kindling to get that potbelly stove going to keep them warm and heat up their dinner. Claire could almost feel that warmth now, cutting through the bone-deep chill of having been in cold water for too long. She could almost hear the snap of those pieces of wood.

No…it was more like a thumping sound. So loud she could feel the reverberations.

Claire's eyes snapped open. She wasn't imagining the sound—or the vibrations. Someone was banging on the toilet door. Why couldn't they open it? Did she have to turn the handle from the inside? Oh, no…she'd locked it, hadn't she? She'd pushed a bolt sideways to secure the door.

She'd have to put her head underwater to reach the lock. Claire felt her heart begin to race. She took a deep breath of the air around her head. And then another, her mind racing along with her heart. Where was the door? Opposite the toilet. If she kept one hand on that and reached straight ahead, she could find the door and then feel for the handle and the button that would shift the bolt out of its hole.

The third breath she took was the biggest and then Claire let herself sink into the water and reached blindly forward to find the door. It took two tries to shift the bolt and then, with her lungs starting to burn from a lack of oxygen, she braced herself by holding the toilet seat and put her feet against the door beside the handle to push. Maybe whoever was on the other side was pulling at the same time because it seemed to open easily. Claire propelled herself upwards then, hoping desperately that the air pocket was still there.

It was. She was gasping to fill her lungs again and again as she felt the movement of another body coming into this small space. With the tank of air on the diver's back, the front of his sleek wetsuit pressed against Claire's body. He spat out the mouthpiece that was distorting his facial features but he was still wearing a mask over half his face and it was so dark in here that Claire had to wonder if she was imagining that she could recognise this person.

No... Somehow, Claire had known who this was from the moment she'd heard the banging on the door.

Or had she just hoped beyond hope that it *would* be Tom?

It wasn't just the lack of space pushing them so close together now. Tom was holding her. Tightly.

'I'm going to get you out,' he said. 'Don't be scared. I've got you, okay?'

'Okay...'

He had one hand underwater and Claire could feel him twisting as he located something. She felt his fingers touch her lips.

'This is a mouthpiece. It's attached to my tank. I need you to seal your lips around it and hold it with your teeth. You can practise breathing with it before we go underwater but we need to be quick. I don't know how much time we've got.'

'But what about you?' How could Claire use his air supply if it put Tom's life at risk?

'This is an Octo—an alternative air source for emergencies. I've got a mouthpiece too. The hose isn't very long, though, so we've got to stay really close, okay? We just need to get out of here and through the cabin and then we'll be safe.' His face was so close to her own. 'I know how scary it is for you to breathe underwater but you're going to be fine. I'll be right beside you.'

That he remembered a snatch of the conversation she'd had with Hanna about how terrifying she'd found breathing underwater was enough to let Claire know how deeply he cared about her.

That he would be right beside her while she did something so scary made her feel far braver than she would have believed possible.

Maybe Tom could see that courage she'd discovered she had because his face softened. As if he was proud of her?

'We need to be careful because there's a bit of debris floating around but I'll keep you safe, I promise.'

Claire nodded. She knew he would keep her safe. She'd never trusted anyone as much as she trusted this man.

She'd never loved anyone as much as she loved this man.

'Just don't let go of me,' Tom warned.

'I won't.'

'Are you ready for the mouthpiece?'

Not quite. Because Claire knew she wouldn't be able to talk once it was in her mouth. She could feel Tom's hand gripping hers. She squeezed it back tightly.

'Don't you let go of me either, will you?'

'Never.' There was a note in Tom's voice that was another promise. 'I'm never going to let you go, my love.'

It was a promise that Tom seemed to be taking quite seriously. He kept a firm hold on Claire as he pulled her out of the space she'd been trapped in and guided her through the cockpit of the boat and then into open water and straight to the surface, where there was blindingly bright sunlight and people and boats everywhere she looked. There was a helicopter hovering overhead. He held her close as he swam towards an official-looking rescue boat and as the coastguard crew lifted her on board she could feel Tom's hand trailing down her leg and holding her foot that had lost its shoe for a heartbeat, as if he really didn't want to lose that contact.

He couldn't hold her physically as he stripped off his flippers and the tank of air but he was still holding her—with his gaze—as she was wrapped in blankets and they were both taken back to shore by the coastguard crew. Other medical staff were there now and everybody involved in the incident was being looked after. An ambulance was waiting to take Claire to the hospital and they both changed into clean scrubs after they'd had a hot shower.

They both went to check on Carl, who had been admitted to the ward for monitoring. He still looked pale and shaken but was doing remarkably well after coming so uncomfortably close to drowning.

'I want you to stay in overnight so we can keep an eye on you,' Tom told him. 'We're going to watch that your oxygen levels are stable and you don't start running a temperature or showing any other signs of infection.'

'But...my boat. I can't just leave it floating upside down out there.'

'It's being taken care of. Someone will come and let you know what's happening soon. Your missus is on her way in as well.'

'And the other passengers?'

'They're all fine, thanks to you making sure they were all wearing life jackets. They were cold and wet but nobody got injured and they'll be telling people about their close encounter with a whale for the rest of their lives. I expect they'll be telling the world about it on the news tonight.'

'What about *you*, Claire?' Carl asked. 'Are you all right?'

'I'm fine.' Claire had to blink back tears. This man had almost drowned because he'd been trying to save her. 'Better than fine. I'm feeling like the luckiest woman in the world right now.'

She caught Tom's gaze. Feeling this lucky wasn't entirely due to simply still being alive. It had more to do with the way he was looking at her and the words he'd said when they'd last been alone together. When he'd said he was never going to let her go.

When he'd called her his *love*...

It seemed as if Tom was remembering those

words as well but he broke their eye contact to look back at Carl.

'I'm taking care of her,' he said. 'Don't you worry about that.'

'Breathe in,' Tom instructed as he held the disc of a stethoscope against Claire's chest. 'And again…'

He looped the stethoscope around his neck. 'Lung fields sound clear,' he pronounced. 'I think you're right and you didn't inhale any water.'

'I'm sure I didn't. I remember holding my breath so long it felt like I was going to burst.'

'And you didn't hit your head?'

He was threading his fingers gently through her almost dry hair, feeling for any lumps or bumps on her scalp. When he saw the way Claire closed her eyes and leaned into the touch of his hands he knew that this examination had just crossed a boundary between professional and personal. And this was very personal. His heart was so full of the love he was feeling for Claire that he had to take a breath. She opened her eyes, his hands still cradling her skull, to meet his intense gaze.

'I thought I'd lost you,' he said, his voice cracking. 'And I knew it was the worst thing that could have happened to me.'

He could hear the way Claire caught her breath. And held it.

'I don't want to lose you, Claire.' Tom's voice was a whisper now. 'I love you...'

He heard the whoosh of that breath being released. It sounded like a mix of relief and...happiness. Joy, even.

'I love you, too, Tom. I just couldn't tell you.'

'Why not?' He was still holding her head, his gaze locked on hers.

'Because... I didn't think you felt the same way.'

'How could you think that, after those nights we had together?'

'It was just a trial run, remember? No strings.'

'The first time, maybe. Not that night in the vineyard. Oh, Claire...' Tom leaned down and placed a slow, soft kiss on her lips. 'That was no trial run. That was...' He kissed her again. 'That was as perfect as it gets.'

'It was.' He loved the way Claire caught her bottom lip between her teeth, as if she felt shy saying that.

'I wanted to tell you that, but... I couldn't.'

'Why not?'

'I thought you wouldn't want to hear it. I knew you didn't want to complicate your life by including anyone else.'

'Oh... I can't believe I really said that.'

'I didn't want you to think you had to give up all the adventures you want to have either. And all the new places and people you're going to find along the way.'

'But I've found the place I want to be.'

Tom could feel the movement beneath his hands as Claire swallowed hard and pulled in a new breath.

'And I've found the person I needed to find. The only adventures I need, Tom, are the ones I can share with you. But...'

'But...?'

Tom's heart sank like a stone. Was he still in danger of losing Claire in his life?

He couldn't understand what he could see in her face because it looked like...fear?

'I'm older than you,' she whispered.

And suddenly Tom understood. Her husband had cheated on her with someone half her age. Had she somehow believed that she was partly to blame? That she wasn't young enough. Or beautiful enough. Or just...*enough*.

How could he find the words to tell her that she was so much *more* than enough?

'You're *you*,' he said softly. 'And you're perfect. Age is...' He gave his head a tiny shake. 'Irrelevant.'

'But you could choose someone young and gorgeous. Like the women Hanna and Kerry were picking out for you on the dating site. Like the woman you met at the café today.'

Tom blinked. 'How on earth did you know that I met someone in the café today?'

'It was a blind date. Hanna got me to help set you up, but I felt bad about it so I was trying to catch up with you before you got there and…and I saw you. And her. And…you looked…happy. When you love someone, you want them to be happy, don't you? I couldn't mess with that.'

'I probably looked happy because I thought you were about to arrive and have coffee with me. If you'd waited long enough you would have seen me escaping with takeaway coffees to go and find Pete.'

'I couldn't stay there and spy on you. And, anyway, that was when Carl saw me and said he had room for one more on the boat and…well… you know the rest.'

'I should have guessed that this was Hanna's doing.' Tom shook his head more firmly this time. 'I'm going to have words with my daughter. She has to stop meddling with my love life, once and for all.'

'She won't need to,' Claire said softly. 'If we make it official.'

'That we're dating for real?' Tom felt his heart skip a beat. 'No… I don't think so.'

He saw Claire's eyes widen in shock.

'This is way more than dating,' Tom said. 'I want you in my life for ever, Claire. I want to marry you. I want everyone—and especially Hanna—to know exactly how much I love you.'

He could see the shadows of doubt in her eyes evaporate. And then he could see what looked like a reflection of exactly how *he* was feeling.

'I can't imagine my life without you, Tom,' Claire whispered. 'Or maybe I don't want to imagine it. I love you. I love you so much.'

This kiss was crossing the boundary for needing a lot more privacy. They needed to get out of here and go home. Tom's gaze caught the tympanic thermometer that was still lying on the bed beside Claire. He picked it up.

'I'd better check your temperature again,' he said, keeping his tone serious.

The thermometer beeped seconds later and Tom frowned at the digital screen.

'Thirty-six point four,' he murmured. 'I wouldn't say you're hypothermic but it's still on the low side. I think you could do with a bit more warming up.' It was hard to stop a smile escaping. 'And you know what they say the best way to do that is.'

He could see that Claire knew exactly what he was talking about. A transfer of body heat. Close contact. Skin to skin. Her smile looked as if it was coming straight from her heart.

'Take me home, Tom,' she said softly. 'Please?'

EPILOGUE

Two years later...

THERE ALWAYS SEEMED to be something to celebrate.

Like Hanna getting into medical school. And how she was loving her studies and doing so well. She wasn't sure that she wanted to end up following in her father's footsteps and being one of the GPs in her hometown, but she was sure that it had been her interference that had brought Tom and Claire together.

'If I hadn't set you up on that blind date, Claire wouldn't have been where she was that day and Carl wouldn't have found her and she would never have been on that boat.'

'Which would have been a good thing, Hanna,' Tom said sternly. 'Claire nearly drowned.'

'And that gave you enough of a fright to see how you really felt about her.' Hanna wasn't about to give up the credit. Her smile could be described as smug, in fact. 'I think I can safely say that my work is done.'

There was a community celebration when *Time and Tide* was relaunched after it had been salvaged and restored. Carl used the relaunch of his beloved boat as an excuse for a party where he and his missus renewed their wedding vows and he got to put his repaired wedding ring back on the finger with its missing tip.

A more private but very special celebration was held of a life well lived, when Mabel Jamieson died at the grand old age of a hundred and one. Claire had seen her only the day before and she'd had tears trickling through the channels her wrinkles had created on her face.

'They say that Livvy's in remission,' she said. 'I can die a happy woman.'

And she did.

But the best celebration so far was even more private than Mabel's farewell. It was the wedding of Tom Atkinson and Claire Campbell and they'd chosen to elope.

'So that Hanna doesn't take over,' Tom growled. 'She might create a website just for the wedding.'

'I'm sure she wouldn't. Won't she be upset to be left out?'

'She can arrange the party for when we get back. We can do it at Beachcombers.' He was smiling. 'Maybe that whale will come back and give us a wave with its tail.'

They exchanged rings in a registry office in Blenheim. They used traditional vows, but when they were alone with a bottle of champagne, back in the little cottage in the vineyard for the night, where they'd truly made love for the first time, they added some of their own.

'I promise I'm never, ever going to take this ring off,' Tom said, holding up his left hand so that the white gold band gleamed in the last of the sunshine.

'And I promise I'm never, ever going to throw my ring into a river,' Claire said. She put her hand over his, so that their rings, as well as their fingers, were touching.

Neither of them was looking at the rings, however. They were caught by each other's gaze and it felt like their souls were touching as well.

They both knew that this was only the first of hopefully a great many celebrations of their love.

This was for ever.

* * * * *

*If you enjoyed this story,
check out these other great reads from
Alison Roberts*

**Midwife's Three-Date Rule
Paramedic's Reunion in Paradise
City Vet, Country Temptation
Falling for Her Forbidden Flatmate**

All available now!

Get up to 4 Free Books!

We'll send you 2 free books from each series you try PLUS a free Mystery Gift.

Both the **Harlequin Presents** and **Harlequin Medical Romance** series feature exciting stories of passion and drama.

YES! Please send me 2 FREE novels from Harlequin Presents or Harlequin Medical Romance and my FREE gift (gift is worth about $10 retail). After receiving them, if I don't wish to receive any more books, I can return the shipping statement marked "cancel." If I don't cancel, I will receive 6 brand-new larger-print novels every month and be billed just $7.19 each in the U.S., or $7.99 each in Canada, or 4 brand-new Harlequin Medical Romance Larger-Print books every month and be billed just $7.19 each in the U.S. or $7.99 each in Canada, a savings of 20% off the cover price. It's quite a bargain! Shipping and handling is just 50¢ per book in the U.S. and $1.25 per book in Canada.* I understand that accepting the 2 free books and gift places me under no obligation to buy anything. I can always return a shipment and cancel at any time. The free books and gift are mine to keep no matter what I decide.

Choose one:
- ☐ **Harlequin Presents Larger-Print** (176/376 BPA G36Y)
- ☐ **Harlequin Medical Romance** (171/371 BPA G36Y)
- ☐ **Or Try Both!** (176/376 & 171/371 BPA G36Z)

Name (please print)

Address   Apt. #

City   State/Province   Zip/Postal Code

Email: Please check this box ☐ if you would like to receive newsletters and promotional emails from Harlequin Enterprises ULC and its affiliates. You can unsubscribe anytime.

Mail to the Harlequin Reader Service:
IN U.S.A.: P.O. Box 1341, Buffalo, NY 14240-8531
IN CANADA: P.O. Box 603, Fort Erie, Ontario L2A 5X3

Want to explore our other series or interested in ebooks? Visit www.ReaderService.com or call 1-800-873-8635.

---

*Terms and prices subject to change without notice. Prices do not include sales taxes, which will be charged (if applicable) based on your state or country of residence. Canadian residents will be charged applicable taxes. Offer not valid in Quebec. This offer is limited to one order per household. Books received may not be as shown. Not valid for current subscribers to the Harlequin Presents or Harlequin Medical Romance series. All orders subject to approval. Credit or debit balances in a customer's account(s) may be offset by any other outstanding balance owed by or to the customer. Please allow 4 to 6 weeks for delivery. Offer available while quantities last.

Your Privacy—Your information is being collected by Harlequin Enterprises ULC, operating as Harlequin Reader Service. For a complete summary of the information we collect, how we use this information and to whom it is disclosed, please visit our privacy notice located at https://corporate.harlequin.com/privacy-notice. Notice to California Residents – Under California law, you have specific rights to control and access your data. For more information on these rights and how to exercise them, visit https://corporate.harlequin.com/california-privacy. For additional information for residents of other U.S. states that provide their residents with certain rights with respect to personal data, visit https://corporate.harlequin.com/other-state-residents-privacy-rights/.